The Introverted Immigrant's Journey

Overcoming Fear, Worry, and Anxiety to Fuel Your Success

Petros Eshetu

Copyright © 2018 by Petros Eshetu

All rights reserved. This book or any portion thereof may not be reproduced or used in any manner whatsoever without the express written permission of the publisher; however, brief quotations may be used in a book review. For more information, please contact petros@petroseshetu.com

Printed in the United States of America

First Edition, 2018

ISBN 978-0-9985548-1-5 (Kindle)
ISBN 978-0-9985548-2-2 (Paperback)

This publication is designed to provide accurate and authoritative information with regard to the subject matter covered. It is sold with the understanding that the publisher is not engaged in rendering legal, accounting. or other professional advice. If legal advice or other expert assistance is required, the services of a competent professional should be sought. Petros Eshetu individually or corporately does not acce responsibility for any liabilities that result from the actions of any pa

Inspired Mind Publishing

This book is dedicated to all my family and friends that have supported me throughout my book journey.

This book is especially dedicated to Helaine Minkus, who is no longer with us, but was such an inspiration to be around. She was the strongest introvert person I knew and set such a great example on how to be comfortable in your own skin and to love who you are, especially as introvert living in an extrovert world. She was kind and had a great heart for everyone, and I'm forever thankful for her contribution to not only me and my family but to the world.

Table of Content

Introduction 1

Chapter 1: The American Dream 6
Chapter 2: The Mind of a Perfectionist 19
Chapter 3: Awareness Is the First Step to Transformation 34
Chapter 4: Adding Meaning to Events 43
Chapter 5: Emotions Rule Our World 53
Chapter 6: Expectation vs. Agreement 64
Chapter 7: Who You Are Right Now Might Not Be Who You Were Meant to Be 73
Chapter 8: Creating Vision 82
Chapter 9: The Immense Power of Intention 93

Conclusion 108
About the Author 112
Review Request 113

Introduction

For the longest time, I asked myself, "What is wrong with me?" whenever I didn't feel like going to parties, happy hour, or simply any large social gathering. The feeling of shame and guilt popped up saying that I didn't fit in into a group.

I felt like I was always on the outside looking in.

What I didn't realize is that it was those same feelings (loneliness, shame, guilt…) that held me back from my success. They held me back from deeply connecting with people, regardless of whether it was a friend, family member, or life partner.

As an introvert (specifically INTJ), I'm comfortable doing activities by myself, but at the same time this approach makes it harder for me to take initiative to interact with others and make more friends.

I tried tricking myself by saying, "I'm an introvert, so I don't need to have many friends anyway," but I was lying to myself. Deep down I wanted and needed more connection.

I always felt like I was "missing out" or not a part of "the gang" ever since I started my working career. I was not making any efforts to reach out because I was afraid of get- ting out of my comfort zone. I wanted to change, but it's not an easy process.

Perfectionism and fear of not being good enough were keeping my life small. I was always apologizing for doing something wrong. I would apologize even when it was not even my fault. It became second nature. I would put myself down so the other person could feel superior; just to make friends.

I wore an invisible mask to hide my true self. That was until I reached a point in my life where I could no longer keep up with different personas/masks I created for different groups. I was exhausted trying to be someone I wasn't.

I was a scared, insecure, quiet person with no idea of who I was or what my passions were. I was in a cycle of self-destruction. A cycle full of anger, hate, guilt, and confusion. It began to affect my life in a negative way, especially with my career and my relationships.

My confidence and self-esteem were at an all-time low.

I finally reached a crossroad in my life. A single event that changed my whole life's direction.

It was after this event that I sought help from mentors and coaches from all over the world to help improve every area in my life—career, relationships, health, and more.

In this book you'll learn how to:

- Identify and kick out any negative beliefs that are holding you back from your greatness
- Connect with anyone easily while being comfortable in your own skin
- Build deep, meaningful relationships while also setting and maintaining personal boundaries
- Set the world on fire, quietly yet distinctively, by using your introvert strength
- Be confident to live the way you were born, embracing your imperfections and reserved nature

- Create a crystal-clear vision of your dream life and make ten times more progress toward your goals

Are you craving connection?

Do you find it hard to connect with family and friends?

For years I struggled to connect with others and I never knew why. Part of the reason for it (most likely) was that I struggled to open up to others due to my lack of vulnerability. I was not willing to show or share my inner world with people so I could avoid getting hurt. Fear was just part of my DNA.

I had many bad experiences participating in social events. I didn't know how to start a conversation and was always nervous of others rejecting me. People could see the fear in my eyes, and I was terrible at reading social cues. All of these bad experiences led me to build a wall to keep others out of my life. I had only a few close family members and friends that I felt comfortable to show my true self without fear of being judged.

As a result, I did a lot of activities by myself, and I loved it. I enjoyed going to a coffee shop and reading my favorite self-help book for hours and hours on end. However, after a few weeks this starts to get old. I began to miss the social connection. I don't like big social gatherings, but at the same time I don't like to be alone too long either.

Have you ever felt this dilemma? It sucks.

I wanted to have a bigger social circle. To get out of my comfort zone and be part of the world rather than just an observer. I was at a point that I was left with no friends. I built too big of a wall around me.

I learned in the last two years that I had a lot of self-sabotaging habits and beliefs that held me back from my greatness. They held me back from connecting with others. I lacked self-awareness on how my negative emotions, fear, worry, stress, and anxiety impacted my life. This lack of awareness influenced all my decisions and kept me from taking risks outside of my comfort zone. To change your life, you need to change your reality. To change your reality, you need to change your beliefs that help create that reality for you.

Purpose of this book

This book is intended to be clear, concise, and actionable. It was designed for introverted folks who want simple, step-by-step guidance in gaining clarity on how to connect authentically with others. However, true transformation starts with connection to yourself first (in other words—your self-worth). Clarity starts by asking yourself the deep, thoughtful questions about how you want your future to look.

I share with you the story of my dream and vision of coming to the USA to start a new life, as well as the challenges I faced and lessons I learned in adapting to American culture—not only as a foreigner but also as a quiet introvert living in a noisy, extrovert world.

I also share lessons and key principles I learned from the hundreds of hours I invested in coaching over the last two years that accelerated my progress to becoming the best version of myself. As a result of that investment, I now make friends more easily, and I'm comfortable going to a room of strangers and connecting with anyone, which before would have given me panic attacks.

This is my promise to you:

I promise, if you follow the guidance found within this book, you will:

Learn to identify and remove negative beliefs that are holding you back from your greatness.

Begin to attract the right people into your life and start building long-lasting relationships by embracing your imperfections.

Learn to create a compelling vision that's aligned to your authentic self and begin to make ten times more progress to- ward that vision.

My mission is to inspire and help you design the masterpiece that is your life. To create your own story of how you want your life to be instead of how it "should be" based on what others think.

Don't delay your happiness for one minute. Life is too short for you to hold off on creating your own inspiration.

Set the example for what you want to see in others. Be the person that people look up to and feel inspired to be like. Let your actions do the talking. Lead by what you do and not by what you say.

The lessons, tips, and strategies you're about to read have been proven to create positive, long-lasting results. I am a perfect example of this. All you will have to do to begin massive transformation is to keep reading. Each chapter will give you new insight, clarifying exactly what you want for yourself.

Take control of your life right now; create your own destiny and enjoy the journey and the possibilities waiting for you on the other side.

CHAPTER 1

The American Dream

WHEN I WAS NINE years old, I had this big dream of one day attending college in the USA. At the time, I was living in Zimbabwe and had been there for a few years. You see, I have a unique background. I was born in Rome, Italy, to Ethiopian parents. My father was working in Italy for a branch of the UN as an agriculture advisor. Then we moved to Angola for a few years. When my dad finally retired, I was seven years old. We moved once again and settled in Harare, Zimbabwe, around 1990.

Zimbabwe is a former British colony and is therefore English-speaking. When I arrived in this new country, I didn't know a word of English and could only speak French and Portuguese after having attended a French international school in Angola.

Zimbabwe was and is a fantastic country to live in, especially in the early 1990s when the economy was stable and flourishing, before it took a downward turn around 1997. At the time, it was the only country in the world where a litre of fuel was cheaper than buying a litre of Coca-Cola.

There are beautiful countryside resorts to visit and many adventures and tourist spots near the mountains and lakes. Every other weekend, my family would travel out of the city to explore the beautiful nearby nature. Despite living in such a great place, I continued to have this curiosity about and urge to visit America.

I watched all the Hollywood movies, like Terminator and Karate Kid, and I got a sense of how life might be in the US. How the other side of the world might look. It was so different from what my life and experiences were.

My favorite sitcom was Friends. There was no satellite TV or internet back then. It wasn't mainstream technology like it is today. I relied on family or friends coming from the US to bring different Friends episodes recorded on a video tape.

I loved Friends not just because it was funny, but I also got to see small glimpses of New York City. Granted, it was staged mostly in an apartment or café setting, but I enjoyed the experience of the characters' freedom of expression and especially their way of life.

The only other way to learn about the American experience was through the exciting stories from friends and relatives that lived there. Many of them went to college and were successful in life. This was when I began to envision myself one day living and graduating college in the US and being successful myself. The seed was planted in my brain when I was nine years old.

I was sold on the American dream.

The reserved, lucky guy

I have always been a quiet, reserved, introvert-type person. However, in my family I was known as the comedian. I loved to make jokes and make fun of myself and others. Humor was always my go-to escape from any problems. It was my outlet for not taking life (or anyone) seriously. I was always being told that one day I would be a comedian.

I was also known as the "lucky guy." Ever since I was little, I always won prizes at school. I would enter a drawing or raffle and would win food baskets with lots of goodies, small money, cakes, etc.

The Introverted Immigrant's Journey

When I was in my late teens, I entered a drawing where the top prize was a free ticket to America sponsored by Ethiopian Airlines. It was part of an event hosted by the small Ethiopian community in Harare. I went that night and bought five tickets.

I remember sitting backstage as the prize winner was about to be announced. I was with my brother and cousins in the back since we were helping with the event. There was no seating available on the main floor, where mostly the older adults would sit. It was close to 10 PM, and a tall man with eyeglasses, grey hair, and a big smile on his face walked to the podium. The gentleman was the director of Ethiopian Airlines and was well respected in the community. He approached the large, brown box that was on top of a table on the stage. After sharing a few messages with the audience, he placed his hand in the box to pick the winning ticket.

The crowd was silent, and everyone held their breath. Anticipation was building with everyone hoping their ticket would be chosen (me included). After what seemed like forever, a ticket was pulled out. Grabbing the microphone with excitement, the director announced, "Number 5-6-2-4-8."

Now, I don't know why, but my heart started racing. I don't know if it was either of excitement or nervousness.

I was sitting in my chair, and I looked down at my five tickets. I scanned them. Boom! There it was! I had the "5-6-2-4-8" ticket.

I was surprised but not shocked for some reason. It's as if I knew deep down that it was my prize to have. It is hard to explain, but I felt destined to win. Instinctively, I grabbed my winning ticket and crumpled the other four. I turned to face my brother and cousins, and told them in a cool, calm voice, "Bye, guys. I'm going to America."

I don't think they heard or processed what I had just said because I said it as if it was not a big deal. Plus, like everyone else, they were still looking down at their tickets, hoping they had the winning number.

I got up and casually walked from the back of the stage toward the director holding the winning ticket. I walked up and handed him my ticket, but I don't think anyone realized that I won. I didn't scream, jump for joy, do backflips—none of that. I just went as if to say, give me my ticket. The room buzzed with confusion about who won.

The director looked at me with a puzzled face as I stretched my arm to give him my ticket. He looked at it, and the expression on his face quickly changed from shock to amazement that I indeed had the winning ticket. He quickly announced, "We have the winning ticket!" The confusion turned to shock that I won, and then a loud applause followed. That was one of the happiest moments in my life. That day brought me one step closer to realizing my dream of going to the USA.

Fast forward a few years later, I moved to the USA at 21 years old, where I started my life and—most importantly—fulfilled my dream of attending a US college.

American hangover

Twelve years on from first arriving the US, I accomplished everything that I had set out to achieve. I graduated from the University of Wisconsin-Eau Claire with a degree in finance and an MBA. I traveled all over the US, including a visit to the "Big Apple" (New York), which was probably one of my best experiences ever. I began a career in finance and worked for some of the largest corporations in the world.

Could I ask anything more? Was my life set?

Now I'm moving on to a new phase of my life—I'm writing books and starting my own business.

Even though I'm living my dream life today—where every day I am waking up with purpose, passion, and clarity—there was a time when I didn't know who I was. I didn't know who I would be. What was my purpose and contribution that I wanted to make to the world?

You see, after arriving in America in the summer of 2005 and then graduating from college four years later, I accomplished the dream and vision I had since I was nine years old. That dream became my reality.

I would sometimes pinch myself to see if it was real. But—what happens next? This was an important question and one I didn't take too seriously at the time, which was a big mistake. I didn't set a new vision for myself. I didn't set new goals after accomplishing my old ones. I had nothing to guide me from within.

After graduation, I began to follow other people's ideas or vision of what I needed to be. I got a job, went into finance, and just stayed there in the corporate world for a few years. I became miserable and unfulfilled in my job, despite getting paid well and living a comfortable life. Looking in from the outside, it seemed like I had everything figured out and had everything I wanted, but honestly, I was lost.

I didn't know which direction I was going in life. It felt like I was on an assembly line, just doing my job and going home. Clock in and clock out.

I job-hopped a lot, hoping to find that "perfect" job that would give me the fulfillment I craved. There was no meaning in my work. The higher and higher I moved up the corporate ladder, the less and less happy I was and the more miserable I became. Even though I hated my job, I didn't know what else to do. All I knew was finance.

Have you had that feeling before? You're in a job you hate, but you don't know what you would love to do next? It's a tough place to be. You're in this strange zone where you dislike your job with a passion, but at the same time, you're terrified of getting fired. It's a no-win situation.

I was confused on what my purpose was. I no longer had a clear vision of my future. My confidence and self-esteem were low. I would get panic attacks with just the thought of picking up the phone or making eye contact with strangers. I blamed everyone else for my problems and how I felt.

Rock Bottom

One day I came home frustrated and annoyed from my day. I could feel my body heating up and neck getting stiff. I put the key in the lock and opened the door of the small 500-square-foot apartment that I shared with my then wife. There was stuff scattered everywhere as we had just moved in. The sight of the mess added to my moodiness, and I could feel my blood pressure going up. I proceeded to go in the bedroom and shut the door, without even glancing at my wife standing in the kitchen.

There was an inner turmoil that was brewing within me, and I could feel I was about to blow. I saw a soft bag hiding in the corner of the closet, and the only thing I could think to do was to kick it as hard as I could to let off some steam. I kept kicking it harder and harder. I was pouring all my anger into the defenseless bag. It wasn't empty, but I didn't care. It must have been a full minute or two before I finally let out enough steam and slowed down to cool off. I had a lot of pent-up feelings that I didn't know how to express. I reached my rock bottom.

The Introverted Immigrant's Journey

Finally, I opened the bedroom door and walked out, only to find my spouse staring at me with a worried look on her face. Not knowing what was wrong or if she did something to upset me.

For months, I had been uncertain of my life's direction. I was trying to figure out who I was. I didn't realize how my behavior all those months had taken a toll on her. I blamed her most of the time for how I felt, which was wrong. I was releasing my anger and emotions on her unknowingly.

At that moment, looking at her disappointed face, I thought to myself, 'What am I doing? Why am I blaming her?' I knew her well enough, and I know deep down inside that she is a kind and loving person.

So, if it's not her, then maybe it's me.

Maybe it's my fault that I'm feeling this way. Maybe I don't know everything. Maybe I' am to blame for all my problems. It must be me.

As I stood there, tears running down my cheeks, I finally realized that I was the person to blame for everything that had happened to me in my life. It's difficult but liberating at the same time.

I had a lot of shame and fear that was holding me hostage from my potential. I was trying to be perfect—a people-pleaser trying to impress everyone, only to suppress who I was inside. I was wearing a mask to hide my true, authentic self so that I could fit in. I followed everyone's vision of what I should achieve and how I needed to live my life instead of following my own path like I did when I wanted to come to America.

I realized that I was unfulfilled in my job and life because I was not pursuing a dream I wanted. Instead, I was focused on what society expected of me. What family and friends expected of me.

The most significant mistake I made was that I stopped dreaming and creating meaningful goals.

I blamed everyone else for how I felt or what was happening. What I needed was to look in the mirror and blame myself. To take full responsibility for my actions. To just say, you know what, I don't know what I'm doing, and admitting for once that I need guidance.

I tried everything that I could think of, everything I learned in my whole life to fix my problems, but those methods no longer worked. I had no clarity on who I was or where I wanted to go in my life. I had so many negative beliefs that were no longer serving me.

What happened to that young Petros who believed anything was possible?

I had negative beliefs that became roadblocks for me, preventing me from taking action on what I truly wanted in my life. I had emotional scars that were not healed.

But once I practiced forgiveness and replaced my negative beliefs with empowering ones, that's when the magic began to happen. I started to enjoy life and see real progress toward my new dreams.

My life began to transform for the better. I felt like a massive weight lifted from my shoulders and an immense pressure was released. No longer needing to be someone I was not; I began to be present in the moment instead of worrying about everything and letting fear take over. I emotionally felt lighter, happier, and more connected with myself and with others. I made more progress in six months than I had in six years.

From a cycle of self-destruction, I moved to a cycle of self-love.

I had to put my ego aside and admit that I didn't (and don't) know everything. Watching a video or reading book or an online forum was not going to solve the questions of this new phase of life I was entering. I needed the right kind of support and guidance.

Seeking mentorship

I looked for mentors and coaches to guide me into a better place and a better way of thinking. This decision completely changed my life.

When I hired my first life coach, I began to work on myself and gain clarity on who I was and who I wanted to become in the future. After a few weeks, my life completely turned around. I began to connect with my spouse and all my friends better. I was happier. My confidence grew. I could now go out and make friends with almost anyone (even complete strangers), which was once so difficult for me. I connected more with people and the environment around me.

I started to see events in my life for what they were and nothing more than that. I gained the courage to be myself. To be vulnerable and to know I'm not perfect. To speak up when needed. To express how I feel in a cool, calm, respectful, and loving way. To forgive myself for the actions of the past that I'm not proud of. To practice self-love and compassion for myself and toward others.

The transformation happened so fast, and what's amazing is I didn't have to move out of state or the country to experience the change. My job and the people I had relationships with didn't change. Nothing changed physically in my body.

All that changed were my habits and the way I looked at my problems. I saw them through a different lens.

The significant change happened in my mind where I saw the world a little differently than I did before.

"If you change the way you look at things, the things you look at change." —Wayne Dyer

I never understood that quote until I experienced my transformation. What was shocking was not the change, but the rate of change. I was accomplishing my life goals, not in a few years as expected, but in a matter of a few months.

Life Coaching changed my life. I thought to myself, what if I could get coaching in other areas of my life where I struggle? Like in areas of improved relationships, clarity in my career, starting a business, writing a book etc.—what would happen?

So, that's what I did.

Clarity on fire

In 2016, I hired coaches from all over the world within different disciplines of life. I wanted to know what my maximum potential was. How much could I achieve in one year?

The more clarity I had on my visions of life, career, relationships, etc., the faster I made progress. I had a fire inside of me to start achieving big things again.

Coaching just added oil to the fire to help me achieve my goals far faster than I could by myself. I had an accountability person. I had someone in my corner who pushed me beyond my comfort level. I had someone who believed that I could accomplish my goals, even though at the time I might not have had that belief in myself yet.

Has that ever happened to you? Where someone else had more belief in your ability than you did for yourself?

At times, you're surrounded by people who kill your spirit to move forward, especially when we want to go for something significant in our lives. All you hear is, you can't do that, be realistic, you're not good enough to do that, you're crazy!

Now, do you have to spend massive amounts of money on coaching to see a massive transformation as I did? Not necessarily, although if you can afford it, I highly recommend the investment in yourself.

That's the reason I created this book—to share the strategies and lessons I learned that led to my transformation.

You see, I noticed one common theme throughout my hundreds of hours in coaching. My coaches helped me to discover my limiting beliefs about my life, regardless of what area of my life I was focusing on. These negative views were holding me back from being who I truly was. I'll share strategies on not only how to identify your negative feelings and thoughts, but also how to remove them and replace them with empowering ones.

I began to create a new vision of how I wanted my life to be.

I no longer wanted to look to others for inspiration, but rather to create my own inspiration. It is the same for you. Why can't you be that guy or girl that others look up to and aspire to be like?

How you do that is by being more (not less) of your true self.

My commitment, based on my journey, is to inspire as many people as I can to be the best possible version of themselves. To help you create a vision that's aligned with your authentic self and your unique gifts, skills, and purpose.

"Nothing happens until the pain of remaining the same outweighs the pain of change." —Tony Robbins

It is my hope that this book will lead you down a path of personal change and taking personal responsibility.

You may have gone through life playing the victim and always blaming someone else for your misfortune. Maybe you blame your parents or spouse for you not pursuing your passions or dreams. Perhaps you blame your boss for you not advancing in your career.

No more.

When you stop blaming everyone else and first look to yourself, that's when you take the power of your life back. When you take full personal responsibility for everything that happens to you in your life (the good, the bad, and the ugly) that's when you begin to make progress.

It may be painful to accept, but I promise you will be a better person in the end. The truth will set you free. You will have the freedom to be whoever you want to be. To create whatever, you want in your life.

Once you stopped being constrained by what society says you should be, you will begin to live a fulfilling life every day, because you will be pursuing goals and dreams that align with who you are.

Final thoughts...

Don't let this be just another book you read and then set off to the side. In some of the chapters you will find exercises to help you get clarity on what you want. Clarity requires reflection and for you to look inward within yourself. For some of us that might be scary, but for others, it's a piece of cake. Whichever end of the scale you fall on, take your time as you go through the exercises.

The only way you will gain value from this book (or any book) is by applying what you learn from the exercises to your life. Some of the strategies and lessons may sound counterintuitive or won't make any sense. That was not by accident, but by design. You may only begin to understand them once you apply them to your life.

The Introverted Immigrant's Journey

It's like driving a car. You can read everything about driving a car, but until you get in a car and drive, you will never understand how it feels to drive.

My promise for this book is that it will help you look at your problems from a new, awakened perspective. Your life challenges might not change or go away, but once you see your problems from a different angle, it will inspire a new way of thinking and perhaps even an "outside-the-box" type of solution if you're lucky.

Albert Einstein said it best: "We cannot solve our problems with the same thinking we used when we created them."

You don't need to travel around the world to be enlightened or move to a new country to fix your problems. All it requires is for you to travel within yourself. The change will happen first on the inside before it occurs on the outside. The only thing you need to change is your mind. Have big dreams; take small actions toward them.

I'm excited for you to read this book, and I have no doubt you will begin to create your inspiration. The fact that you reached this point lets me know that you want something more from life. It will be an honor for me to be a part of that journey through this book.

CHAPTER 2

The Mind of a Perfectionist

I WAS ALWAYS A perfectionist and a people-pleaser. I made sure I never made a mistake in front of people. I had to look the part to blend in easily in groups. If I hadn't done that, then I saw it as a failure. I failed to meet the expectations of others. Of course, I was unable to reach these false expectations I had of myself. The possibility of being rejected by the group was terrifying.

Sounds silly as I think about it now, but this was my mindset for most of my life.

It all started in second grade. I was one of the only chubby kids at school. I stuck out from other kids like a sore thumb and was always the target for other kids' teasing.

It's funny now thinking about it, but I was the target of kids that were smaller than me (you would think it would be the other way around). The bullying was not physical but more psychological.

I recall one teacher in second grade calling me a "fat, useless boy" after I made a mistake on my homework or classwork. I still remember how painful her words were back then, and they stuck with me.

I never felt lonelier than I did in primary school, even though I had a twin brother (Paul) who would back me up if anything happened. In the classroom, Paul spoke on my behalf since he knew I was always quiet and not the type to speak up. If the teacher asked me a question,

Paul would answer. Eventually, the teachers placed us in separate classrooms so each of us would speak for ourselves, and I would hopefully break out of my shell and speak up more.

Always a quiet and reserved person, the continuous bullying made me distance myself from others even more. I stayed in the background of group settings or activities. From my second-grade experience (around eight years old), I incorporated a belief not to stand out as I went about my life. My goal was just to blend in and be like everyone else. To wear an invisible mask and hide my true self.

This is how I went about life for a long time—in my head I associated standing out with pain. I tried my best to fit in any way that I could. This became especially crucial upon my arrival to the US in 2005 to start college. To fit in I wore the same clothes as other students. When I went for job interviews, I dressed like the other candidates. At times, this is a good strategy but sometimes it's not, because I didn't express my true identity.

A fear-based mentality motivated all my actions.

You will always be consistent with the identity you create for yourself. If you have empowering beliefs, you will have confidence and high self-esteem. However, if you have negative beliefs, then you will not think highly of yourself or your abilities. I was ashamed to be myself, to be different, and with that fear came anxiety and low self-esteem.

Even years later—after I finished high school and I was no longer that fat kid—I continued to carry the mindset, belief, and fear of the fat kid. Do not to stand out or else the pain of rejection will come my way. This was ingrained in me as part of my belief system. Just because you get older or you lose that weight, doesn't mean that your earlier beliefs disappear.

I bring this story up because both you and I developed some limiting beliefs from our childhoods that make up our self-images. Some of these beliefs are holding you back from your greatness. They're holding you back from doing work that means something for you.

What are beliefs?

Beliefs are merely the way you experience the world. A belief is a statement of your view of reality that feels true to you.

How does one create a belief? Some are learned from others, and some we developed ourselves.

The best way to explain it is to think of your mind as if it's a new computer. You have the hardware, but no software installed. You add programs for the computer to function well. It's the same with your brain where you "download" beliefs to interpret your experience of the world around you.

The beliefs you download can be either good or bad. They can lead you to success or hold you back from it.

Beliefs can be self-sabotaging, meaning they can hold you back from taking a risk that could possibly improve your life or get you closer to your life's goals.

Beliefs like "I'm not good enough" or "I'm not special" are very common statements we tell ourselves to prevent getting out of our comfort zone. Think of these statements like a computer virus—you don't even know it's there until the problems show up.

Beliefs can also be empowering. Maybe you learned them from your family. These can be beliefs such as, "I can do anything I set mind to" or "Always give your best and never quit."

Both positive and negative beliefs are treated equally in our minds. The only difference is that one holds you back while the other pushes you forward.

For example, has there been a time in your life where you felt like a failure?

Perhaps you failed at a project when you were young. You may have felt the guilt and shame of being a failure. It stuck with you until this very day. This one event that happened years and maybe even decades ago can still affect you.

Perhaps someone you highly respected a long time ago once told you that you weren't good enough and it's been stuck with you ever since. Maybe the person who told you that you're not good enough, meant to say those words in the context of a particular moment in which you didn't put in much effort.

As a child, especially between birth and seven years old, we don't have that level of understanding and awareness of time and the difference in deciphering who you are as a person vs. who you are within that moment.

Now as you go about life to work or want to start a business, you ask yourself, "Can I even pursue that idea?" Then that little voice in your head responds with a negative belief, "Hey, don't you remember when you failed to complete the task last week or years ago? How can you possibly run your own business?"

You confirm, "That's right, I'm not good enough." You feel fear and anxiety come in to do its part. Even if that person who told you this many years ago is no longer living, you still feel it.

This dialog happens so fast (within a millisecond) in your mind, and we have practiced it so often that's it's a habit now. If a significant opportunity comes your way, your automatic response is "No, I can't!" And you make up an excuse to not do it.

It has happened to me so many times. I always wanted to be a writer but held back. In school, my English teacher would tell me how terrible my writing was. After all, English was my third language, and at nine years old I was already insecure about speaking it, let alone writing it. This was always in the back of my mind. It was only once I changed my beliefs about myself that I began to make progress in my book writing years later in adulthood.

Before you move forward, let's further define beliefs and how you know if you have a contrary belief.

The best way to know if you have a negative belief is to look at your results. What goals did you set this past year? Have you made any progress on them? If not, why do you think that is?

Have you been blaming someone or a situation for why you are not moving ahead?

What if I told you that you are your own obstacle to your success? That's it. It's not your parents or spouse or whoever you think might be holding you back. It's you. You have control of your destiny. Remember what I told you earlier, this book is about taking personal responsibility. You can lie to everyone, but you cannot lie to yourself.

You're either "in the way of" or "on the way to" your best life.

So again, I ask you, why do you think you're not making progress on your goals?

Take a moment and sit with it.

Go somewhere quiet, remove all distractions (laptop, phones, etc.), and ask yourself, why am I not getting the results I want?

Sit back and see what thoughts pop up.

Obviously, this won't be a straightforward process for everyone. For some people, they are attuned to their thoughts and how they feel, while others find it difficult and have thousands of random thoughts coming at them at the same time.

Take your time and do what feels right for you. However, make sure you do it. Self-reflection is a key step for transformation.

Discovery of my belief

I discovered my negative belief regarding meeting new people or trying to make more friends only after I talked about it with my coach. I had a goal to expand my social circle and connect more with like-minded people. However, for whatever reason, I never took action on that goal for the past few years.

My coach assigned a small task to meet people and introduce myself at a local event, but I was terrified. To go to the event and just introduce myself? That's just not me. But I didn't want to let my coach down, and I wanted this change that I kept resisting.

I also wanted to sit at home and read my favorite book quietly. That's my comfort zone. But even that gets old, and I wanted to experience life.

I discovered the reason I was not accomplishing the goal of meeting new people was that I feared rejection. Up until that point, I didn't even know that I had this belief from my childhood. As I talked with my coach about my experience, it dawned on me that I had a belief that I was not good enough. Why would anyone be interested in listening to me? I'm not special, and no one cares.

I kept repeating in my head, "Plus, I'm introverted, and I don't need a lot of friends." In other words, the very small group of friends I have is enough. My thoughts only justified me not wanting to leave the house and meet people which fed the negative belief. The truth is, I was lonely. I was no longer living like in my college days where I got to meet different people and learned new ways of seeing the world from other perspectives.

I went to the event anyway, and guess what? It wasn't as bad as I thought. I prepared some conversation starters, but my goal was just to go and introduce myself. I ended up making connections with a few people.

If you have a goal or task and you're just not moving forward toward it, then there may be a limiting belief in your mind that you're not aware of yet. I learned that you can have all your goals written down, have the picture on your beautiful vision board of accomplishments you want, but if you have a limiting belief in the back of your mind, you will not reach those goals.

I believe in the power of coaching to help in whatever areas of life you want to improve or goals you want to achieve. My coach helped me to be accountable and could catch self-sabotaging thoughts I had toward myself. Now I've expanded my circle of friends far and wide. Some of them I have met at events and even some online groups. I belong to different online communities where I can add value to the group and vice versa.

Are negative beliefs all that bad?

Despite the bad experiences (rejections) in my earlier days at school, I learned new skills from that negative belief that ironically helped me prepare for my future success.

You see, not standing out meant that I joined groups where I was more of a listener than a talker in both one-on-one and group settings. People that appear annoying or unbearable to others are somehow easy going with me. To be honest, I simply didn't take what they said personally. I just learned to be patient and listen.

Lots of people enjoyed my companionship because they had someone to talk to. They would reveal things that they didn't share with others. They felt comfortable around me and knew that I would not judge them. They were the Yin, and I was the Yang. I was their silent interpreter of their feelings. I could reflect how they felt better than they could themselves.

I learned the value and power of being understood, which is so important to everyone. Everyone wants to be heard and have their feelings acknowledged. To know they are not going crazy and that somebody "gets" them.

You can eliminate shame and suffering by first acknowledging it.

Nowadays, many of us tend to go on social media and rant about how we feel, but it's never as comforting or productive as having another human being actively listening and understanding you. To connect to another person rather than a device.

Even though everyone came to me and felt at peace, I was not understood in return. I held back in sharing my inner self (again it's that invisible mask role-playing from fear of rejection). I was kind to everyone but myself.

Does that happen to you? Are you so forgiving of others but not forgiving of yourself?

It's as if it's okay for others to make mistakes but not you.

So, my belief helped me become a better listener and to show empathy.

Your strength now becomes your weakness

Even though I lost a lot of weight by the time I reached high school, I still had the mindset of "I'm not good enough" and "Don't stand out, just blend in."

My body and situation changed, but not my mindset.

Later, after college, this belief took a toll on me. I was stressed, overworked, and exhausted from keeping up with the different masks I wore with different groups of people. Trying to have a different persona with different people is difficult, especially at work when you're communicating with different groups within the organization daily.

I was always a follower in everything I did, but as my career progressed, I was forced into situations where I had to be the leader of a team or a project. As a result, it never worked out well, because in the back of my mind I still had the belief not to stand out or else the pain of rejection was coming my way. Without realizing it, this thinking had held me back for years.

In my finance jobs, I was in constant communication with many people in the organization. It was exhausting keeping up with the different personas I created. The "blending in" strategy, as I call it, was proving to be difficult. The people-pleaser approach was getting old.

I reached a point in my life where what was first seen as a strength (the "blending in" approach) was now a weakness. It was holding me back. It no longer worked. It no longer served me.

What led me to my past success was now the lead to my future failures. Everything was crashing in on me, and I didn't know what to do.

I didn't know how to fix it.

So, I just did what any normal person would do. I kept doing the same thing repeatedly and hoping for a different result, only to be disappointed every time.

Thus began a cycle of self-destruction. I felt like I was a hurricane going round and round, banging into things everywhere. I lost my footing. I was stressed, miserable, and running on empty.

I was running fast to nowhere.

My self-esteem took a deep dive and was in tatters. My motivation was at an all-time low.

Instead of stopping to reflect and make a meaningful change, I kept moving forward like a stubborn bulldozer. This led to building upon my perfectionism even more, which served only to feed into the cycle of negativity, fear, and insecurities.

In the coming chapters, I will discuss more on how to change this negative cycle, but first I want to share the power of travel and the effect it has on beliefs.

Travel opens you up to new beliefs

"To travel is to take a journey into yourself." —Danny Kaye

Being an Ethiopian who was born in Italy, grew up in Zimbabwe, and later moved to the USA, I've been fortunate to have experienced many different cultures, values, rituals, and beliefs. I had the opportunity to travel around the globe, including many parts of Africa, the USA, Canada, southeast Asia, Europe, and the Caribbean islands. I don't know why, but travel is what I love the most and is the best teacher of my life. It's when I travel that I do my most reflection in life.

If you think there is only one way to approach your problem, you can go to another area of the world that will have a completely different take on that same problem.

Many people I have met in the U.S. are scared to cross the Pacific Ocean, especially if it's to a Third World country. They have a fear of not knowing what to expect on the other side of the world. The news always reports negative stories from outside nations, which for the most part is exaggerated. I know this because I also was a victim and was brainwashed by that nonsense.

In the USA, I would look at the news about Zimbabwe, which always got negative press. Being that I have friends and family that still live there, I naturally worried about them. I will never forget the day I read something online about some issue happening there, and I immediately called my mum to ask if everything was ok. She was puzzled and responded back saying everything was fine there. She had no idea what I was talking about.

At that moment, I realized I had been watching the news so much that I forgot that I lived in Zimbabwe for fifteen years. I know how it is, and I know the stories will always be negative about this country due to difference in politics with the West. I got sucked into it and was getting programmed to be scared to go back to the place I grew up. I now realize why people, especially the many Americans I meet, are terrified to travel outside the US. Who can blame them? I would be too—and, for a moment, I was.

The clash of cultural beliefs

To say I had a culture shock after arriving in the US would be an understatement.

I remember my first day of college at the University of Wisconsin-Eau Claire in August 2005. I had arrived in the USA about a month or so prior. I was excited and nervous to enter the classroom, not knowing what to expect. My palms were sweaty, and my heart was beating fast. I had to learn how to speak and interact with American students. It was a small campus with six thousand students or less, in a small town of sixty-five thousand.

I had to learn how to speak up in a classroom and even possibly go against the professor's ideas or teachings. To know it's okay to debate with the professor and question him or her. To have a questioning mindset.

This was very different from what I experienced back home, where as a student you listen to teachers and don't openly question them.

Also, elders are highly respected in our society and are seen as more important than the younger generations. But in the U.S., everyone is treated equally. Even addressing adults by their first name was difficult for me to wrap my head around, because back home you will get slapped in the head to think you are at the same level as an older person. It just doesn't work that way.

That's not to say that one culture is better than the other, it's just different. It takes some getting used to. When you spend your whole life thinking one way, and you realize there is another way of seeing things, it requires an adjustment in your belief.

Different cultures have different beliefs that create different realities on how to live life. No one cultural belief is more right or wrong than another.

Depending on where you live, you might need to take on different beliefs to adapt to that society. It doesn't mean you abandon your old beliefs or values, but to be open to a new way of seeing the world through other people's eyes.

Think of it as adding a new belief into your repertoire. Like adding a new skill to your resume. Nothing happens to your old ability; you just have more in your arsenal of knowledge.

Travel is a great teacher—you will realize that we are more alike than not with people everywhere. I honestly believe that if people travel more, they will be less discriminating and have fewer prejudices toward others who look different from themselves, which I think is fueled by fear.

In the end, everyone in the world wants the same thing—to be happy, to be loved, to be respected, and to have food in their stomach.

So, you might be wondering, what is my point with all this?

Well, it's this—beliefs are different for everyone, and you can change them anytime you want. You don't need to be married to them. To change them just requires an open mind to new things and experiences.

Negative beliefs need to be removed and replaced with empowering ones, but at the same time, you can also keep adding new beliefs along the way. It doesn't mean that your current positive beliefs are wrong, but there's always room for more that are different than your current ones.

Consider if you were born in another country—you would have a completely different set of beliefs than what you have now. This doesn't even include beliefs and values you picked up from your family's household, which may or may not be different from the beliefs tied to the local culture.

For example, if an American child is born and raised in China, he/she will have some Chinese cultural beliefs as they blend into that society. Also, vice versa, if you have a Chinese child who's born and raised in the U.S., he/she will grow up with some American values. Beliefs are all interchangeable and not tied to you.

Just think about it. The beliefs you have right now, regardless of religion, family, or career, would be so different if you were born in another part of the world or born to a different family.

"I would never die for my beliefs, because I might be wrong." — *Bertrand Russell*

Final thoughts...

Beliefs can take different forms. You may have childhood beliefs that are still resonating with you. Some of those beliefs are empowering you to be the best person you can be, while other beliefs might be holding you back from your full potential.

At times, you have a belief that may have benefitted you in the past but is no longer needed in your life. Don't be afraid to upgrade.

Fear keeps your mind and your life small. It holds you back from the potential for you to be greater than what you are now. Just like when I expanded my world through meeting new people and traveling, you can do the same too. Fear keeps our world, thoughts, and lives small.

The first step to happiness and fulfillment is first changing your reality, and to do that, you need to begin to change your beliefs.

Beliefs can be changed with open-mindedness to how you view the world.

My hope is that you now have a better understanding and awareness of beliefs and how they impact your experience.

CHAPTER 3

Awareness Is the First Step to Transformation

HOW DO I CATCH myself on my own limiting beliefs?

That is like asking a fish if it knows that it's swimming in water. It doesn't know until you take it out and it begins to suffocate. Same with limiting beliefs—you don't know you have them until you start to see the same negative results over and over, and frustration and anger kick in.

Has this ever happened to you?

You start your day with a list of tasks you want to accomplish. You're pumped up, feel good, and happy to finally remove some items from your ever-growing to-do list. But the day goes by, and you get distracted here and there. You're juggling multiple priorities, and every- one is stealing your time away from your important work.

If it's not one problem, it's another.

Next thing you know that day is over. You return home exhausted and tired, and you sit on the couch only to feel frustrated, stressed, and annoyed all at the same time. Meanwhile, your to-do list is still long, and, if anything, it has grown longer because of the lack of progress. You're disappointed in yourself, and you know tomorrow your list will grow, adding more anxiety and worry for you.

You have goals you want to reach in your life, but it seems like your actions don't align. You may be productive during the day, but are you efficient?

Are you moving closer to or further away from your goals?

Are you doing activities that seem easy and fun, instead of those that are harder yet necessary?

Do you have clarity on what your priorities are? Is it that you don't have enough time, or you're not organized? Could there be a fear of failure in the back of your mind?

This happened to me so many times. I would set a goal to improve my relationships and increase my social circle. Then as days went by, I would go to work, come home, and hop on the computer, doing everything but working on my relationships.

Even at work, I wouldn't put much effort into building a strong bond with my team. I'd do just enough to complete our projects. That was until I talked to my life coach, whom I will call Mike for privacy reasons.

Mike asked me clearly, "What is your goal this year?"

My response back then was, "To have more enriched relationships in my life."

He replied, "What have you done last few weeks to move you closer to the goal?"

Me, "Nothing."

I ended up giving him excuses that I didn't have the time or some other reason.

So, if I set a goal and I haven't done anything about it, then why set a goal in first place? Do I need to change it?

Deep down, I knew I didn't need to change my goal, because I always felt lonely and wanted to meet new people. However, I also knew something else was going on. But what?

After further discussions with Mike, I realized that I had a deep fear. A fear of rejection.

Despite the awareness of my belief, I still needed to take action to have a transformation. The minute I was aware of the thoughts holding me back, I acted and reached out to people in various groups. This was way out of my comfort zone, but I was willing to take the rejection or no get a response back. What's important is I tried.

In the end, many responded back, and I ended up building strong relationships with the people I reached out to. When I was looking for a career change into the marketing area, I used a social media site like LinkedIn to reach out to people within my geographical area that had the marketing background that I was looking for and invited them for coffee. Again, I was so out of my element and I didn't think anyone would respond, but surprisingly many did and were willing to help. The first two coffee meetings were nerve-racking, not knowing what I would say. Eventually I got over it, and after a few meetings I knew the type of questions to ask. It's all trial and error.

The only way to replace a self-sabotaging belief with a new one is to act. For me, it was to take initiative and reach out to people. Acting helps you associate the positive feeling with this newly added belief.

I used to hate networking (especially as an introvert), but I now enjoy it. I've learned so much from the people I've met, and I've even received job offers through networking.

Coaching buddy

Hiring a coach or finding a mentor is another way to increase your awareness in whatever area you want to work on. I can't tell you how helpful having a coach by my side was in supporting how I evolved from who I was then to who I am now. I had so many unhealed wounds from the past that I was bringing with me to my future.

As I mentioned, in one year I hired six or seven coaches to support me in many areas of my life and spent hundreds of hours working with them. It was not a low-cost decision to do so, but it has been the greatest investment of my life. I never realized I had so many beliefs that no longer served me. My coaches guided me, held me accountable, and gave me honest feedback on how I could improve in specific areas of my life.

I learned a lot of principles that I still apply in my life today. For example, from my writing coach I learned to first connect with my readers and then communicate my solutions to whatever problem they are facing.

The feedback I got from my coach took my writing skills to a whole new level. I also finished my book in three months having no prior writing experience before then. I got help and developed a roadmap of the do's and don'ts of writing. In addition, I received support from someone who's already spent hours making mistakes. I got to learn from my coach, and save days, weeks, months, and even years of procrastination.

Now, having said that, if you have someone you trust who can be a mentor for you and guide you in the field you are heading into, great! The point is to try not do things on your own, especially if it's a new area you're heading into.

Awareness Journal

"What is necessary to change a person is to change his awareness of himself." —Abraham Maslow

From my experience, journaling is the key to increasing your awareness of a struggle you're facing. I talk more about this in chapter five. Whenever I feel stuck in a problem or a challenge, I pause and sit with it. You can do this as well.

Ask yourself why you are not getting the result you're looking for. What am I doing wrong? What can I change? What can I not change? Sit with it for a few minutes.

The answer will eventually reveal itself to you, and you can start writing down what comes to you. Just write and don't judge what you're writing at the moment, simply let it flow.

You may discover you're not making more money because of a self-sabotaging thought like rich people are bad or money is evil, so every time you try to make more money, you self-sabotage because you don't want to be that type of person. I've heard of people who fear making a lot of money because they will then earn more than their parents which might change their relationship.

Maybe you're a woman, and you have a belief that all men are cheaters and can't be trusted (vice versa for men not trusting women too). That belief, whether knowingly or not, will self-sabotage all your future relationships even if you do meet the most loyal guy or girl. Whenever you get close to your dream person, you will find a reason to mess it up just so you can prove that you were right in what you thought.

Keeping an awareness journal will help to bring these thoughts and beliefs to light so that you may address them and replace them with positive thoughts and beliefs.

My weight-loss experiment

I recently joined a weight-loss program to get healthier and lose inches from my body. I have struggled to lose weight since I was a kid.

Part of this weight-loss program was to eliminate dairy and grains (bread, rice, pastries, etc.) from my diet for three months. This seemed extreme, especially since bread has been part of my diet from a young age. I thought, how do I survive without it? Plus, stopping grains will mean I have to stop eating my Ethiopian staple food, enjera. Enjera is a very popular flat, spongy, pancake-like bread served with spicy sauces and meats.

It was hard to start the program because I had been eating these foods since I was a kid (for thirty-something years). However, nothing was more painful than to sacrifice my biggest pleasure in the world—peanut butter. Peanut butter was my go-to food whenever I felt down or simply needed something to snack on. I began to track how I felt before, during, and after my meals. On a given day, if I had cheated on the diet, I would reflect and write down how I felt before eating it. Was I hungry or craving it?

Have you tried to start a diet, and at the first sign of temptation you start telling yourself, I will begin the diet after I eat this or that?

Anytime I started a diet, and I saw a delicious cake or other treat on the weekend, I would tell myself, "I can start my diet on Monday."

Maybe you worked out that day and told yourself that you deserve a treat, so you got donuts or a burger.

Does that sound familiar? I know I sure am guilty of it. Where do you think you learned this from?

For me, I learned when I was younger that when I behaved or did something good, I would get a treat. My parents would get me candy, ice cream, pizza, or whatever junk food that I wanted. I also would be able to treat myself to a soda, which was a big deal back then since the only time I got to drink soda was on special occasions.

It's no wonder I always self-sabotaged when I tried to lose a significant amount of weight. I would treat myself to sweets and eat cake, only to regret it later and feel sorry for myself. The guilt set in, and I would tell myself, "I won't lose weight anyway, so what's the point?"

Then the "I'm not good enough" belief kicked in to justify why I wouldn't lose weight. That just triggered me to eat my peanut butter like always because it brought me good feelings and comfort.

This was a never-ending cycle.

It was only once I began to write down how I felt every day with my food experiences that I began to see a pattern. I started to be aware of what I was thinking in the moment before deciding to eat anything. It takes a lot of work and self-reflection, but it eventually pays off.

Whenever I messed up, I would reflect on what I did wrong and how could I improve tomorrow. I forgave myself thousands of times and tried to get back up as quickly as possible and not feel bad too long.

After three or four months, I lost fifteen pounds. The inches kept dropping from my waist and all around my body. It was a fantastic feeling. My face got thinner, my complexion improved, and my skin began to glow. I slept better and had more energy throughout the day.

I felt amazing and had to go to the retail store every three months to buy smaller clothes.

This could only happen once I became aware of my self-sabotaging beliefs. Once aware, I began to make different decisions on what to eat. I learned to pick different kinds of healthy foods and learned to cook new recipes. I also ate out less as a result. More importantly, I finally began to get in touch with how I felt about certain foods. Just because a food smells or tastes good doesn't mean it's good for you. Also, vice versa, just because a food doesn't taste good doesn't mean it's not healthy for you either (like raw vegetables).

Our cultural beliefs can also stop us from making progress. I used to think because I'm Ethiopian I must eat enjera—it's part of my culture. Then I questioned if this was is true. Am I genetically predisposed to eat enjera? What happens if I reduce how often I eat it or just stop completely? Well, I found out—nothing bad happens. In fact, I feel much better. Enjera simply filled an emotional void in me and reminded me of being back home with my family and enjoying our time together like the old days.

So just because you're Italian doesn't mean you must eat lots of pasta, or if you're Asian you must eat lots of rice. Even though it's part of your culture, be open to new ways of seeing food.

Final thoughts...

I encourage you to do a lot of reflection. To be still and ask meaningful yet powerful questions of yourself like, am I happy right now?

Your mind is like an online search engine. If you ask yourself a good question, it will search deep within to give you an answer. If you ask yourself a lousy question, well that is the kind of reply that you can expect—lousy.

Why am I not getting the result I want?
Why am I not losing weight?

Why am I not surrounding myself with the right people?

That's why I encourage you to journal how you feel or how your day went. Think of journaling like talking to your best friend. It's therapeutic and you understand what you think about the most throughout your day.

The power of journaling is that it increases your awareness of what is going on in your mind. You often don't even know what thoughts you have until you write them down. You may be shocked at what you see on the pages (or if you're typing, on the screen).

If you accomplished something on a day or felt disappointed in a situation or how you reacted, write it down. Journaling is a great way to acknowledge how you feel and move past it.

What led to you feeling this way?

What triggered that negative emotion from you?

Most likely, there is a negative belief playing in the back of your mind without you knowing it.

Once you understand what's going on, you get another chance to make it right tomorrow. You can plan for a better outcome.

Always remember to forgive yourself and have self-compassion, especially if the day doesn't go as you expected or you don't meet a goal. Dust yourself off and start fresh the next day.

CHAPTER 4

Adding Meaning to Events

"It's not the events of our lives that shape us, but our beliefs as to what those events mean."—Tony Robbins

HAS THIS EVER HAPPENED to you?

You got rejected by either a company, or a project, or even a group that you wanted to join, only to question your self-worth. You tie yourself so much to the outcome that anything less than success is a failure.

Maybe you tried to fit into a group where you just weren't accepted and felt a huge rejection. Then you believed that something must be wrong with you. I know, because I felt like this all the time at a certain period in my life.

You see, I attached meaning to events. I interpreted my stories to go along with how I felt. If I didn't get that job, it must be that I am not good enough, or if a group didn't accept me, that must mean I'm not good enough to hang with them.

Now as I look back, these statements were untrue and hurt my motivation and self-esteem. There are many reasons why things happen, and it's not always the reason you think it is. It most certainly has no meaning to it unless you assign one.

Suffering through our own created stories

Everyone has suffered at one point in his or her life. I learned that most of my suffering came not from the event itself, but the meaning I gave to it.

When you begin to tell yourself, "XX happened, so that must mean I did YY," you are setting yourself up for negative feelings like disappointment, rejection, resentment, and more.

"He/she didn't call me, that must mean he/she doesn't care about me." "I didn't get the job, that must mean I'm not good enough."

"I failed this project, that must mean that I'm failing as a person."

For me, for almost every adverse situation that happened in my life, I always took them personally—a rejection of me. When my friends didn't want to talk to me or did not respond to my calls or messages, I would take it personally. I would feel bad, guilty, or even ashamed during these situations. I ended up feeling negative towards them, even though their lack of response had nothing to do with me but just them or their availability.

I kept playing the victim game. I looked at everything from my view, and not once did I ever stop and try to see things from the other person's perspective.

He/she didn't call me because she was busy, or it was bad timing, or he/she was just upset about something.

I didn't get the job because someone internally was hired, or position was already taken, or the manager didn't like the red tie I wore or one of my jokes. Who knows?

I failed because that project or job was not a good fit for me and did not utilize my strengths and gifts to my full potential.

I wish had known all this back then; I went about life feeling rejection everywhere I went.

The feeling of guilt, shame, and anger was a constant cycle of emotions that crept up continuously throughout my day. That was until I saw a video that forever changed my life.

How a twenty-minute video changed my life

I watched a short video that forever changed the way I saw myself. It was a TED Talk that I just happened to come across as I was browsing online. The speaker was Brene Brown and presentation was called "The Power of Vulnerability." You might recognize her NY Times bestselling books, Daring Greatly or Gift of Imperfection. She talks about how you go about life carrying the shame of not being good enough, so you try to perfect yourself in front of others and not show your vulnerability.

I immediately related to it. Her words spoke to me powerfully, as I never allowed myself to be imperfect in front of anyone. I cared so much about what others thought of me and never realized that it's okay not to be perfect. After all, if you're perfect, why would anyone want to be around you. You'd just remind them of how imperfect they are. How can anyone relate to you? How can anyone connect with you at any level without some common ground?

The power of vulnerability was such an eye-opener and a shock because I never saw myself that way. I began to cry with this huge realization and new awareness. Brene spoke to me about how I was feeling for a long time.

I never knew a video could have such an impact on me. That day I remember just sitting back in my chair and reflecting on everything that happened to me in the past. How I never understood why things turned out the way they did. Why people, strangers, friends, and family treated me in a certain way. Just differently. I always could feel something was wrong, but I never could put my finger on it.

I just took it as "I'm not good enough," or "I'm not perfect enough." I had stopped allowing myself to open up to others, so it was hard for others to open up to me.

Now everything made sense. I began to put the puzzle together of past conversations and events that never made sense at the time. But it hit me, and I understood why things happened as they did. I was relieved, sad, hurt, and disappointed as I thought back to situations or relationships that could have been so different (better), if I knew all this back then.

After that video, I began to open myself up to people. I would say 'no' to requests that I couldn't meet and set boundaries on what I could and could not do. I no longer feared the consequences of my actions but went with how I felt and what made sense. I used to take on a massive workload at work because I didn't want to say no and look lazy or imperfect.

There was always a constant fear of "I will get fired if I don't do this." That's the limiting belief I had, and it led to stress and resentment for the job. I expected to get an adverse reaction from work colleagues on my new change, but surprisingly, nothing happened. When I said 'no' to people, they just went and found someone else to do their work.

Of course, they weren't all happy, but life moves on. I don't need to feel shame every time I get a request that I can't do on someone else's schedule. There were a few people that tried to make me feel guilty for my change of approach or not doing a task. It might have worked in the past, but things had changed. "Petros got his groove back!" I consciously began to respect myself, and my colleagues followed suit.

When your ideas fail

"Failure is simply the opportunity to begin again, this time more intelligently." —Henry Ford

Failure, or rather the fear of failure, is the most prominent block to progress. It's not failure itself that's the problem because everyone has failed in something at one point in life. But it's the meaning we add to it.

What lesson did you derive from the failed experience?

Did you take failure as a reason not to try again, or did you see it as just bump in the road? A nudge to redirect you into a different path. I was one of those people who felt if I failed, then it was a sign that it wasn't meant to be. I would sulk for a few days and go over everything that went wrong.

Failure was always hard for me to get over because I tied my self-worth to the outcome. If I pursued an idea and I failed, I interpreted it as if I failed as a person. For example, I had this business finance idea that I wanted to help people with their budget and finances. I set up a website, logo, and all the social media accounts. I made the website colorful and fancy. But after few months I got no traction or people visiting the site. I tried asking family and friends, but nothing worked and there wasn't much interest. I was sad and disappointed.

I didn't know why my idea didn't work.

Then I stopped to ask myself, "Do people even want this service?"

Months later, I realized I made the #1 rookie mistake for any entrepreneur. I failed to do market research before I invested money in a fancy website. I later realized nobody was going to pay me to manage their budget because there were a lot of online tools that allowed you to do it for free or at a minimal cost. I felt stupid for not seeing this and dropped the idea.

It was tough the first few days after that failure. It was my first attempt to become an entrepreneur, and it was a disappointment. I fell flat on my face (so to speak). I told myself it wasn't for me. For months, I felt sorry for myself.

Then one day I watched a speech by Les Brown, a well-known motivational speaker. It was an hour-long video. He repeated a phrase that stuck with me, and I could not let go of it. He said, "If you fail, make sure to fall backwards, because if you can look up, you can get up."

Wow! That was exactly what I needed to hear at that moment. I realized how I was stuck in my head for a long time. I kept repeatedly blaming myself for the failure. Then I thought, what good is it to feel sorry for myself and do nothing? Just move on. So, that's what I did. I finally broke out of my failure trance.

I decided to take action and dust myself off. I hired a business coach to help give me a roadmap to properly start an online business. I learned that it's okay to fail and just take the lesson. I acted on my next idea of starting a career blog to help people transition into their career. It didn't do as well as I would've liked, and that's okay, because I knew I was headed in the right direction. I'd adjust and try another path.

I began to change my associations and beliefs about failure. I now see it as a lesson to re-adjust my strategy. Before, it would have devastated me, but now I'm more accepting and know it's all part of my journey.

Don't worry, be negative?

I had to ask myself, "Why is it that whenever an event occurs in our life, that our natural default is to attach a negative meaning?"

Why is it not positive?

I have a theory about why we are negative in our first reactions. It all starts with the saber-toothed tiger story. My theory is that, as humans, you and I are wired to look at the negatives in our surroundings. This is based on our ancestral background where we needed to focus on the negative rather than positive in our environment to survive and be aware of the dangers that threaten our lives including our family's lives.

Way back when our ancestors lived in communal-type villages, the villagers had to watch out for animal predators that came close to the village looking for prey. That concept or instinct of watching out for danger is still genetically ingrained in us. We are always on constant lookout for danger, whether it be the environment or people or animals we meet.

Could this explain why negative news always captures more people's attention than positive? I believe there is some connection.

Just look at the news channels. For instance, watch and see how they will focus more on how many planes have crashed, which are relatively few, compared to how many planes have landed safely, which are by the thousands per day. It's as if we focus on the tragedies around us so we can be aware of the dangers and know what to do or avoid in the future.

Stepping out of your boundaries

The most significant challenge you and I face most often is getting out of our comfort zone. You may prefer to stay in your comfort zone than to risk something new. To illustrate this, let's stick with the saber-toothed tiger story.

You see, our ancestors knew not to go beyond the boundaries of the villages and away from the community. They didn't know what might await past those limits.

Was the saber-toothed tiger waiting to grab someone? Were there other animals to watch for?

There is this fear of the unknown if we cross outside your walls. Fear of leaving the village boundaries was what kept everyone alive. Being part of a large group and sticking together has power. This is the mentality or human instinct we have right now, especially whenever we want to try something new.

What if I start this business and I fail? Or succeed?

In other words, what if the saber-toothed tiger comes for me? Should I even try to go out and see what is beyond the wall?

I remember when I was writing my first book all kinds of fears popped out. What if no one likes what I write? I had to be vulnerable and reveal things about my life that only a few people knew. Again, I am a reserved and private person, so this was way past my comfort zone. Would I be judged? Would I be rejected by family/friends and not be accepted for sharing my ideas and beliefs?

I ended up launching my book, and I never expected that it would get the reception it did. Lots of people congratulated me and recommended my book. They felt inspired by the stories I shared. I ended up getting an interview on national TV in Ethiopia and a few podcast interviews. I got so many emails from people who were inspired by my story. I never would've imagined that it could turn out the way it did.

But I had to step out of my comfort zone to see what was on the other side of my wall.

There were many times I was getting close to my goals, only to begin to sabotage myself. I would complete 90% of my book and start telling myself, this is not a good book, let me start over. It is a bad idea. Who will read my book anyway? As it turned out, many still do.

I share my story to remind you that fear always comes in when you get out of your comfort zone, and that's okay. It's there by design (not by accident). It's for your protection. But if there's something you want in your life, you will need to take a risk and step outside of your boundaries. As Lisa Nichols, a well-known motivational speaker, most famously said, "Success and comfort don't live on the same street."

Our ancestors needed to go hunting for food, or else they would go hungry and starve. Eventually, they had to step out of their safe zone to hunt for animals.

Was there a fear they could encounter a big beast that could kill them? Yes. But there was also an opportunity to kill an animal and bring it back to feed the village.

At times, you may be hungry for your dream. To lose that weight, start that business, change your career, write that book, etc. Everything you want is waiting for you on the other side of your comfort zone.

You can starve with your dreams and not do anything, or you can live a rich, fulfilling life by taking the risk and attempting to make them your reality.

"Shoot for the moon because even if you miss, you'll land among the stars." —Les Brown

Final thoughts...

Remember, events are just events. Nothing more and nothing less. You can't control the events, but you can control how you react to them.

Once you begin to understand this, you will start living in the reality of "what it is" rather than "what it should be."

You'll stop tying your self-worth to the outcome, and instead learn from every failure and success. You'll take rejection for what it is and not add meaning to it. Failure doesn't mean you failed as a person. It's a signal to adjust your path.

When I began to see events for what they were, my suffering and stress levels dropped significantly, and I began to have more happiness and joy come into my life.

So, what about you?

Are you attaching yourself too much to the outcome vs. focusing on the learning?

What meaning do you give to an event that either happened or is happening in your life? Now ask yourself, is it true? What POSITIVE meaning can you attach to the event?

In the next chapter, we will talk more about emotions and how they control every decision we make in our lives, whether we realize it or not.

CHAPTER 5

Emotions Rule Our World

"When dealing with people, remember you are not dealing with creatures of logic, but creatures of emotion." —Dale Carnegie

I REMEMBER ARRIVING AT Minneapolis Airport and then taking a connecting flight to my destination on a small plane that could fit maybe ten passengers. That day there were only six of us.

Each person was seated in a specific section of the plane so that the aircraft remained balanced throughout the flight (yes, that's how small the plane was). I started wishing I had chosen the alternate shuttle option to the campus as I felt vulnerable in the air in such a small aircraft.

On the flight, I could not relax. It only took a slight gust of wind to shake the plane. It was scary and nerve-racking. I was gripping my seat, holding tightly to my armrest for my dear life. I felt fragile in the air. It was turbulent during the whole thirty-minute flight to my new city. By the time I arrived, I was exhausted, and my ears were ringing from all the noise on the plane.

That was my experience arriving into my new city. Turbulent. What I didn't know then, was that "turbulent" would describe my first two years in the USA—turbulent and shaky. I found it hard to adjust. I was this quiet, introverted guy who landed in a world where extroversion is highly valued.

The Introverted Immigrant's Journey

It was hard to make friends early on, as I was shy and self-conscious about how I spoke and did not want to stick out. It's difficult enough when you're one of a few African (black) students on campus, let alone in the whole city. I also had a British sort of accent, which only increased my standing out. Zimbabwe was a former British colony, hence the reason I had a trace of a British influence in the way I spoke.

Everywhere I went, the moment I spoke, people would ask where I was from. The first few times it was great to hear that people were interested to know where I was from. But then it became a daily thing. Everywhere I went, I'd be asked. It became tiresome quickly.

The reality was I couldn't change my skin to blend in, but at least I could adopt a US accent to stick out less. I tried to learn and observe how other students spoke and picked up a few phrases along the way. As I made friends with other students, I quickly learned how to speak American-style English fluently

I missed my family, friends, and community back home. It was difficult to share my experience with other students since most of their families were a mere twenty to thirty minutes away, while mine were thousands of miles away on a completely different continent. We didn't have Skype, WhatsApp, Viber, or other types of communication apps back then (in 2005). In fact, I didn't even have a cell phone for the first two years on campus. I would use the land line in my room.

My response to the loneliness in this new land was eating lots of food to calm my sad emotions. I had a food culture shock (if that even exists). Back home there were not as many food options at the grocery stores as compared to those in the USA. For example, I only ate Cornflakes for breakfast back home, but here there are Honey Nut Oats, Fruit Loops, Frosted Flakes, Cinnamon Crunch and so many more. So many delicious choices with different colors and flavors.

Before bed each night, I would eat a muffin. I had never had one before coming to America. When I went to eat in the cafeteria, which was buffet-style, I filled my tray with lots of delicious food. Since I ate alone most of the time, I had no shame in stuffing myself with the extra food I grabbed.

We tend to numb/medicate ourselves when we are unhappy, feel empty, not worthy, or ashamed of being who we are. I overate. I thought that my only escape from this feeling of emptiness was food. "Comfort food," if you will.

Has there been a time in your life where you felt lonely or low? When you felt alone and lacking in self-love?

I bring this story up because not being aware of your emotions can hold you back from what you truly need in your life.

Emotions are there to signal to you what's going on with you now. If you're not aware of your emotions, you can sabotage yourself as you try to move forward in life.

There were a few students that reached out to include me in activities, but I was in such a negative headspace that I ignored them. I preferred to stay a victim, plus my ego (the self) was not willing to reach out for help. I was sadly comfortable in this world of victimhood.

The understanding, awareness, and management of my emotions was the most significant factor for my transformation in my life and reaching my goals.

Humans are emotional creatures, and almost every decision you make in your life is determined by your emotions. Whether you know it consciously or not, your emotions govern your life.

You may find this chapter to be the most important one in this book. It is the acknowledgment of your emotions that will allow you to let go of your many past wounds and scars that are holding you back from living your best life.

Emotions are strong signals from deep within you that indicate a message or call to action. They are part of our human essence, our instinct. Your gut, intuition, or just a "feeling." They are the source of your happiness, health, and anything fulfilling you want in your life.

How to make decisions – Do I use my head or heart?

When I talk about the heart, I'm not talking about the physical organ that beats thousands of times a day and looks like an upside-down pear. I'm talking about your gut, your intuition. The first instinct reaction that you have to something.

Whenever you're unsure about a decision, always get in tune with how you feel. In other words, go with your gut. Remember, emotions are faster than intellect. What I mean is the heart is faster at making life-changing decisions than your logical reasoning (your head).

At times, you might make a gut decision that feels right, yet is scary and on the surface level looks unwise, but as you look back months or even years later, you realize it was the right decision. It's all about perspective. For example, I remember when I quit the finance job where I felt unfulfilled and miserable in. It was scary. I didn't know what would happen next.

Where would I get my next paycheck?

What did I want to do next? I was confused and nervous.

I knew what I didn't want, but I didn't know what I did want. Have you ever experienced that?

Being caught between a rock and a hard place, is a frustrating place to be. On one hand, you want to move forward, but on the other hand you don't know how or which direction to go. It is paralyzing.

I was at a place where I was not happy in my life and was stressed in my job. Part of me wished that I would have approached quitting my job differently and tried to work out the issues. However, the other part was glad that things turned out the way they did because that break from my work allowed me to get clarity about what I wanted in my life.

The day of discovery for my passion

I discovered my passion by accident. It all started with a conversation I had with my life coach, that I will call Brad for privacy reasons.

Brad told me about a retreat that his organization does once a year in Provo, Utah, that he thought I might like. It was a three-day event with other like-minded people who value personal development.

I thought it sounded awesome, but the two-thousand-dollar price tag seemed a bit costly, so I told him I wasn't sure if I could go.

He responded that it was still a few months away and that I had time to think about it.

Two weeks later, I met up with Brad for our regular coaching session call, and he asked if I had thought about the retreat any further. I told him I wouldn't be able to afford it.

Brad was cool with it, not at all pushy.

Then he said something that completely puzzled me.

He said, "Let me resend you the email again with information and the event link."

I don't know why, but something in me shifted at that moment. I thought to myself, I already told him I'm not going the last few times we spoke, but he still felt the need to resend the information.

My gut said just look at the email again.

As I read the email later, I got this sense that I needed to go on this trip. I didn't know why I felt this way.

Then I told myself I didn't have enough money, and I didn't want to go into credit card debt for this trip.

However, the urge to go didn't go away. I kept envisioning myself going and taking in the Utah mountain scenery.

My heart (my intuition) was telling me to go, but the negative self-talk came in to interrupt me. Deep down, I knew it was the fear of the unknown that was holding me back. What will I gain from this trip anyway? Do I risk it?

Have you ever felt that way? Where your heart tells you one thing, but your mind is telling you something else?

I talked with my friends to get his thoughts on whether I should go for the trip. His response was, "Just go with how you feel."

Of course, this was a foreign idea for me since I was not used to deciding how I felt before making a decision. I tended to use my rational/analytical thinking. I felt my decisions should make logical sense.

Is the cost worth the benefit?

At that moment, I wasn't sure what the benefit would be other than seeing a new city and meeting new people. After thinking about it for a day or two, I decided to take a chance and go.

I was nervous as I took out my card out to purchase my ticket and book my flight. I felt a tension on my neck as if I was getting strangled and choked for every penny I had left in my bank account.

A few weeks later, I arrived in Provo, Utah. I reached a cabin located on the mountainside near where the Sundance Film Festival is held. During the three-day retreat, I met lots of people, including a special guest who inadvertently changed my life.

This guest was a successful person in his own right, an entrepreneur, multiple bestselling author, and the leading star of the successful movie, The Secret, that brought the law of attraction to the mainstream world. It was none other than Dr. Joe Vitale.

As I sat outside in the beautiful sun, overlooking the mountain with white snow at the peak and a waterfall halfway down the one side of the mountain range, Joe Vitale began to share his story about how he started out, long before the fame and success. It was a typical rags-to-riches story, but very inspiring nonetheless. His love for books is what caught my attention.

Joe loves reading and writing books. In fact, he has written sixty-plus books, most of them becoming bestsellers. As he spoke about his passion for books, I felt a jolt of energy rush through me. I connected with his passion and everything he said. I kept repeating in my mind, "That's me! I'm the same way." I felt like I just found my new best friend.

It was at that moment that I realized that I was meant to be a writer. In my mind it was now a fact; I am a writer.

I remember Joe telling all of us at the retreat that you can be holding your book in twelve weeks. At first, I didn't believe that it could happen. However, somehow, I believed in him. I believed Joe when he said it that it was possible, and that I could do it.

Have you ever had someone else believe in you before you began to believe in yourself?

After the retreat, I flew back to Minneapolis with a new energy and purpose. I didn't realize it back then but going to that retreat forever changed my life's direction.

What's crazy is I didn't even plan it.

I didn't know what to expect before going there. I was nervous and had so much hesitation. I was stepping out of my comfort zone. I knew we would do activities and meet new people, but never in my wildest dreams did I think I would get this new, enlightened awareness of myself and my gift to the world.

For you, it may be a different path. But the only way you will know is by experimenting and going out and meeting people. When you connect with someone at a deep level on what they do, you will know it. You will feel euphoric inside. You just know.

Whenever you must make an important decision in your life, and you're not sure what to do, follow your gut or intuition. Be mindful of the negative self-talk that creeps in to keep you from taking a risk and trying something new. It stems from a fear of stepping out of your comfort zone. If I listened to that fear, I would not be here writing this book and living this happy, fulfilling life and waking up with a purpose every day. I must pinch myself at times to see if this dream life is real.

Some decisions don't always make rational or logical sense at the time, yet it may be the right choice to make. Don't get me wrong, I'm still analytical when making decisions, but I have learned to let it slide every now and again.

I was lucky enough to discover my passion right after I quit my stressful and unfulfilling job. Is it a coincidence? Maybe or maybe not.

I was so caught up in the busyness of life and mundane routine that I needed to take a break away from everything and just let go. To take a breath and understand what direction I wanted to go in my life. I had to step out of my comfort zone to discover what else is out there for me.

Looking back, I always thought that I discovered my passion by accident, but that's not true. What I realized was that I always knew deep down that I was a writer, but I didn't have the courage to admit it to myself and own it. It's as if I needed permission to go for what I wanted and to dream big.

Final thoughts...

I believe that the ability to manage your emotions is the biggest predictor of success.

This is the secret to massive transformation. Humans are emotional creatures. Nothing gets done without emotions getting involved.

For the longest time, I wasn't aware of my emotions. All the rejections were making me feel negative, angry, embarrassed, and ashamed.

This eventually led to me being fearful to be myself and of trying anything that's worth risking. It led me to eat a lot of food to suppress my difficult emotions, so much so that I ended up being overweight (weighing over two hundred pounds). This held me back all those years from doing what I truly wanted and kept me in my comfort zone.

Fear is there for your protection but don't let it consume you, especially if your life is not at risk. It's probably just a signal that you're going out of your comfort zone.

Now, managing your emotions doesn't mean ignoring or avoiding your negative feelings, but instead, it's embracing how you feel.

Accept and acknowledge how you feel without judgment. Sit with it for a short while. Are you happy, angry, sad, etc.?

You want to become aware of how you're feeling throughout the day and journaling it (yes, journal it). By writing down how you feel, you will print it in your mind. It will increase your awareness of how you are feeling at that moment.

That increase of awareness is an essential step to transforming your life. Most of us are not aware of how we feel every second of the day. I didn't for the longest time. After all, how can you fix something that you can't see? This was my big 'aha' moment.

When I began tracking how I felt throughout the day, I began to see a pattern of tasks or activities that made me fearful and that I was avoiding.

I would discuss my daily journal notes with my coach, and slowly we began to address my self-sabotaging beliefs and replaced them with new ones that empowered me versus knocking me down.

I started taking small actions toward each of my goals. I began to upgrade my relationships—I slowly removed those people that were dragging me down and made me feel bad about myself instead of lifting me up.

In the past, whenever I was annoyed, ashamed, or angry, I would just suppress my feelings and try to ignore them with the hope they would disappear. This was obviously the wrong approach. What I needed to do was be aware and acknowledge how I felt. To acknowledge it to myself or, better yet, with someone I trusted to share it with.

I began catching myself when in a bad mood and would take a break, take deep breaths, and pause. I would allow myself to sit through whatever I was feeling and let it pass.

Exercise:

- How do you feel when you go about your day? What emotions are you currently experiencing?

- If you don't know, start journaling your experiences. For example, every day at noon you can stop whatever you're doing and just pause. Ask yourself, how do I feel now?

- What emotions do you want to experience throughout your day?

- Which activities or people give you the most joy and happiness? How can you incorporate them into your life more and remove those activities (or people) that drain your energy?

CHAPTER 6

Expectation vs. Agreement

Expectation leads to misery, while agreement leads to creativity.

> *"Expectation is the mother of all frustration."*
> —Antonio Banderas

I CONSULTED FOR A large corporation a while back, helping them out with their analytics. It was the end of the day on a Friday, and I was about to clock out for the weekend.

I felt the energy and excitement in my bones—with a huge smile reaching from ear to ear, I was ready for the upcoming weekend where I planned to go out to the lake and relax.

Just as I was about to turn off my laptop, I got an urgent message from the manager telling me to call her ASAP.

I thought, uh-oh, what did I do wrong this time?

But then again, I knew it didn't take much to rattle her feathers, being that she was a detail-oriented and micro-managing type of boss.

I reluctantly called her to see what was going on. She picked up the phone and immediately I could tell from her tone of voice that she was not happy.

I was hoping for the best but preparing for the worst.

She informed me of a mistake I made on my analysis, which I needed to fix. I thought to myself, "No biggie; I can fix that in a few minutes." To my surprise, however, she had already sent the final analysis to her boss without reviewing it and giving the final approval.

This mistake was obviously embarrassing for her and me for not catching this error earlier. Taking full ownership on my part of the error, I apologized and told her I would fix it right away.

Suddenly, with no warning, the conversation took a turn for the worst. Her responses came back like knives.

"How could you make such a mistake?" "You are too incompetent to do this job." "Why can't you be as good as so-and-so?"

It was shocking, and I felt blindsided. Our relationship had always been one of mutual respect. It had never reached a point of verbal attack before.

It's never a good sign when a manager compares you to another person. I had been working there for three months, and she was comparing me to a person who had been with the company for ten years. Even if we had worked there the same number of years, everyone is different in their approach. At that point, her expectation of me was unrealistically high and unreasonable, especially when compared to a more tenured person.

However, I learned in life that when people come at you with over the top anger or confrontation, whether it be because you cut someone off in traffic or accidentally skipped the grocery line, a lot of times that anger has nothing to do with you and everything to do with themselves.

It is something in their own life that they are not happy with or angry about, and you happened to be there to trigger it (often at no fault of your own).

It's just like using a pressure cooker to cook hot broth. Your anger builds up, and eventually, the pressure needs to escape. Unfortunately, I happened to be the escape valve that day.

We hung up the phone, and I was angry and disappointed with how it ended. My heart was pounding so fast that I felt it was going to jump out of my chest. I had never been treated like that in all my work history.

I'm a very quiet and calm guy in nature and rarely react to most situations. But there is a line in any relationship that you should not cross, and it just got crossed.

What happened next, you might ask?

Well, I fixed the error like I said I would and sent it back to her. I then sent a second email informing her of my immediate resignation and explained how I felt about the inappropriate way she handled the call and the situation.

In the past, I would have taken the verbal abuse from a manager and just let them walk all over me. I would feel inferior to their power status. But thankfully, those days are over.

The manager had a high expectation that was not realistic for someone who just joined the company. The manager would likely never be happy with my future work, and I would be the one stressed, knowing that no matter what I did, my work would never be satisfying.

Has someone had an unrealistic expectation of you?

Instead of asking if you can do (or handle) the work, they just assume you can. How do you feel when that happens? Do you feel angry, bitter, unappreciated?

This is very common not only in the workplace but in our personal lives as well.

Comparison

Have you ever had a family member place an expectation on you to do something or be a certain person? They might say something like, "I'm disappointed in you, I expected better from you," or "I expected you to be an engineer or doctor, but now you're just a..."

Even worse, they compare you to your siblings or other family members, saying, "Why aren't you more like your cousin or brother/sister? At least he/she got an 'A' on that subject or is working this or that job. What went wrong with you?"

Sound familiar?

You want to ring their necks and shake them like a tree until all their leaves fall off their head, and they get some common sense. How many times did you want to respond back sarcastically, or state the obvious that of course you're not like so-and-so? Each of us are unique in our own way, so to compare us makes no sense.

At times, I have wanted to respond to those types of comparisons by turning it around on them, asking why they aren't like the favorite uncle that gives better gifts, or another comparison that would ruffle their feathers. I have never done it, but I think that might drop the comparison conversation quickly.

Expectation vs. Agreements

Building and maintaining relationships is essential for you to have a successful and fulfilling life. You can approach or build relationships either through agreements or expectations. I hope you guessed by now which one leads to a land of loneliness, frustration, and anger. Yes, that's right—expectation.

A boss setting unrealistic work goals without completely understanding an employee's situation is a typical example. Maybe the employee doesn't have the resources, the knowledge, or the time to complete a task.

Setting expectations without asking a person if he/she can meet the deadline causes added pressure and leads to resentment from the person performing the task. Asking someone whether he/she can meet your demands/expectations allows them to add their input to the decision-making process and leads to agreement.

As mentioned earlier, I have been guilty of setting expectations myself. When I was in college, I was driven to do well and get high grades in my classes. So, when it came to group work, I always approached it as if everyone wanted to do well and get top grades too (putting forth their best effort). I realized painfully that another person's drive is not necessarily as strong as mine. It's not to say they didn't care about the work, but their priorities were different.

A good stereotypical example is this—if you're married, maybe your wife expects you (the husband) to take out the trash or bring in the income. If you're the husband, maybe you expect your wife to clean up the house and take care of the household. This is old-school thinking. These are expectations that we might have learned from our parents growing up. It may have been the norm a few decades ago, but the younger generation doesn't need to follow their elder's expectations of marriage. Things can and should change, including our mindset.

Now, if you talked to your spouse and made an agreement to divide chores or other life duties accordingly, then you will have a better chance of getting along and avoiding unnecessary conflict or misunderstanding based on an old set of beliefs.

What worked for your family growing up doesn't mean it must be what you do with your new family. When two partners come together, they form a modern culture in the household that is unique to them. They must make agreements as a foundation for building this new relationship. It doesn't have to be an agreement on paper; a verbal agreement based on trust can work.

When you think about it, a lot of us sign agreements often, such as when applying to rent an apartment or a car loan application. Why? To make sure both parties understand what is expected of each other and to avoid misunderstanding.

Do agreements work for group settings?

The answer is YES!

I learned this from group coaching. I've attended countless group calls from different coaching programs. After participating in a few, I noticed that every time I started with a new group, we had to agree on what was expected of each of us. Different group calls had unique agreements at the beginning, but the foundation was the same: that we all participate in the discussion, be honest when expressing how we feel, and were always encouraging and respectful to each other.

Our coaches could have just set an expectation on all of us and moved on (hoping that we would follow). That probably would not have gone well, especially if individuals were not able to meet the expectations for whatever reason. The group calls usually went well because we had a manifesto for each group, and we had an agreement to fall back on whenever anyone did not pull the weight in the conversation or was acting inappropriately. This helped reduce group conflict and held us all accountable.

Benefits of agreements

"Unless both sides win, no agreement can be permanent." —Jimmy Carter

In case it's not already obvious, agreements are powerful. Everyone loves agreements because they're a win-win for both parties most of the time. Every day you must negotiate in life, whether it be a work project, pricing negotiation, or even to negotiate with kids so they can do what you ask—for example, "Eat more spinach now and you can watch cartoons after."

Everyone negotiates, and it's always better when you have an agreement between the two parties. I remember telling my young nephews (two boys, ages five and seven years old), "No cartoons until you eat your food." They would rebel, protest, and throw a tantrum. When I realized this approach was a struggle, I decided that I needed a different approach. I then told them that if they eat their food and finish it, I would take them to the park or they could watch their favorite show. Wow, what a difference that made. I never saw kids eat so fast.

Final thoughts…

Expectation is a one-way street, while agreements are a two-way street. Agreements allow for more creativity because your brainstorming how to meet each other's needs. It's more fun. Once you give your word, that word is a bond. Rarely do you see people make commitments with the intention of disappointing the other.

So, what happens when you go around setting expectations all day long? Disappointment and resentment. Expectations without agreement are probably the biggest reason that I suffered in my relationships and why I was in a cycle of self-destruction for so long. I had expectation from and of my friends, coworkers, and even strangers (which thinking about it now is crazy).

When I began to remove my expectations of people, that's when my relationships started to improve. I began to have deeper, more authentic connections with others. I learned to go to an event or situation prepared but with no expectation except to be fully present in the moment, and to let things unfold and deal with whatever came to me at that point. To be present and be a good listener without judgment. This is not an easy task, and I'm continuously working on improving myself in this area.

"For me, a life without expectation results in a life with inspiration."
—Alanis Morissette

Exercise:

Below are some questions to reflect on.

- Reflect on a time where you were disappointed with something or someone. Maybe it was someone who said they would help you with something but never showed up. Maybe you expected excellent tasting food from a fancy restaurant, only to be disappointed with the quality and service you received. How did it make you feel? What feelings other than disappointment did you experience? What thoughts came to your mind?

- Have you ever set expectations on others? Was it a realistic expectation?

- Have you had a conflict in the past with someone? Could the reason be that you both had different expectations of each other?

- Knowing what you know now, how would you have approached your past conflict with someone?

CHAPTER 7

Who You Are Right Now Might Not Be Who You Were Meant to Be

THIS IS ESPECIALLY TRUE as I go into offices where I see people drag their feet along the floor as they walk in the hallways. Emotions cease to exist (or at least heavily restrained). All I see is routine, a cycle of boredom and misery on their faces, and their body language screaming for new life and adventure.

I know this very well because I was one of those zombies at work. Then I asked myself, "Do I love this job?"

Since I was young, I was always told that I could be whatever I wanted to be. Most of us are told this. You know, the typical, "Whatever you do, set your mind to it, and you can achieve it."

As much as this is true, did you know what you wanted to do in the first place? Maybe you wanted to be a pilot or a firefighter when you were younger but as you got older, you were steered into a career path that was not chosen by you but for you. That safe and "respectable" career—engineer, accountant, doctor, lawyer…

Who can blame you?

That work identity was ingrained in your beliefs since you were younger by well-meaning parents, friends, mentors, or teachers. After enough repetition over the years, you identified yourself with that profession before you even began the job.

Who you are right now might not be who you were intended to be.

If you're not energetic or excited to go to your job (or about your intended field), then you might need to ask yourself why.

Could it be that your career is not aligned with your authentic self and naturally gifted skills?

According to a 2016 Gallup study, 51% of US employees are not happy in their jobs. There could be many reasons for this low percentage, including toxic work environment, bad company culture, ineffective management, etc.

However, I believe the reason for this lack of engagement is due to people being "stuck" in a job that does not utilize their unique skill set.

Reality check

"Working hard for something we don't care about is called stress. Working hard for something we love is called passion."
—Simon Sinek

The truth is not all of us are born to become writers, public speakers, doctors, engineers, preachers, etc. That is, of course, unless you love and enjoy working in these professions. If so, then keep rocking it. But for everyone else, you need to keep fighting that good fight and begin to seek out and pursue your true passions.

I don't say this as a discouragement to not go for what you want, but more of an encouragement to go for a career that aligns to you—not what somebody else told you that you should be. Only you can determine your path.

Anybody can be a speaker, but not everyone will be great at it. Some people love talking to large groups and performing in a lot of collaboration-type activities. There are other people (like me) who prefer one-on-one activities that can utilize their unique problem-solving abilities. (I'm talking to the introvert folks here.) Don't get me wrong, I enjoy being part of a team, but when it comes to digging into a problem, I prefer doing it by myself with no external pressures.

For example, Tony Robbins is a most popular motivational speaker and coach. I read he found his gift early on when a high school debate teacher noticed how good he was speaking in front of the classroom. He enrolled in a school debate competition and won it confidently. This was an early sign of Tony Robbins's gift for public speaking and influencing people on stage.

This is not to say that you cannot learn or add new skills to your inventory, because you can and need to. After all, it's important to learn skills like public speaking even if you're an accountant or writer. It will improve your communication skills with your audiences, readers, or clients, especially if you hope to become a leader in your field. However, make sure your major focus is on developing your unique skill strengths and add complementary skills as needed.

What if I dedicate enough hours to my craft? Can I still do what I want?

Personally, I think you can work hours on end on a certain skill area, but if it's not aligned with your unique abilities, you will only reach a certain level of success. You will be good but not extraordinary compared to someone that thrives with that skill set.

For example, Michael Jordan was an amazing basketball player. During his successful career, he decided to switch sports from basketball to baseball. This was so he could fulfill his dream of being a baseball player.

Michael Jordan applied all his hard work, talents, and skills to this new sport. Despite giving it his all in this new area of his life, he realized that he would never reach the heights of success as he did in basketball. He learned to appreciate his gift and talent that he had for basketball. He soon quit baseball and finished his career back in the NBA.

Another example from my personal life—I have always been good with numbers, so I went to college to study finance because I didn't know what else to do at the time. I graduated and had a finance career for a few years. I'm good at it but if you were to ask me if I loved it, I would say no.

I don't wake up in the morning excited to crunch numbers or calculate investment returns for companies. It doesn't excite me now, and I don't know if it ever did. However, I have had work colleagues who love finance. They look at financial news and the stock market whenever they get a chance. Their energy and enthusiasm for numbers are through the roof. That's when I realized the difference between liking a job vs. loving a job.

However, there are other benefits to working in a job that's not in your field of interest, like improving your skills in communication, leadership, team collaboration, conflict resolution etc. Just have an open mind and see what works best for you.

You don't hate Mondays; you hate your job. You don't love Fridays; you love life.

Everybody knows the key to living a fulfilling life is to follow your passion. I have always heard, "Follow your passion! Just do that, and everything else will work out." Some people say that's good advice, while others say it's bad advice.

It's so confusing. Which one is it?

Plus, how do you follow a passion when you don't even know what that passion is?

I kept asking myself these questions repeatedly. I have too many passions, which one should I pursue?

Have you ever faced that dilemma?

How do you know which passion is worth going after?

You won't honestly know if one is worth pursuing until you try it.

Understand, however, that sitting and thinking about these questions all day won't get you anywhere.

I was tired of not being fulfilled in my job.
I was tired of feeling helpless.
I was tired of feeling stuck in a rut, knowing I had so much potential to do more.

I realized I needed to stop thinking and start doing.

You get clarity only once you take action. You may travel one path that will lead to a dead end. You take another route and you move closer to your passion. That's how life is.

So, are you following someone else's dreams instead of your own?

Passion is a journey

As much as this sounds cliché, it's true. Discovering your passion is not a destination, but a journey.

This applies to everyone. Yes, including you!

Also, it's worth noting that you can't find passion outside of you or in a specific type of job or work. It is an internal journey from within yourself.

What do I mean by that?

Well, many times I was stuck in my head, thinking for hours and days on what my passion and purpose might be. What I later learned was that my brain was not designed to answer that sort of life question.

Passion has to do with how you feel and not how you think. How do you feel when you do a certain task? Are you happy and energetic or do you feel drained from the activity?

Does your job light you up, where you can do it for hours and hours on end ?

"There is no passion to be found playing small–in settling for a life that is less than the one you are capable of living." —Nelson Mandela

Find your unique GIFT

In my previous book, I Came. I Saw. I Jumped!, I discussed how, instead of focusing on following your passion, that you try following your GIFT.

What is your gift?

Your gift is that unique skill that you have. Each one of us was born with a unique gift. It's something you're good at that others struggle with.

What do people compliment you on all the time or come to ask you for advice about?

Maybe you get compliments like, "Thanks for organizing the dinner party last week," or "Thanks for connecting me to Jane from the medical device company." Or perhaps you get questions like, "How do I invest my money wisely?"

A perfect example of someone who profited from her passion is Japanese consultant Marie Kondo. If you don't know her, she is the author of the NY Times bestselling book, The Magic of Tidying Up, that talks about her method of cleaning, storing, and organizing your home. At an early age, she learned that she loved organizing people's homes. At 19, she started getting paid to organize people's homes and started her own consultant business. She had so much success organizing, that she wrote a book that has sold millions, and she was listed as one of Time's "100 most influential people" in 2015.

So, what unique gift do you have that you can profit from?

Here are three strategies that you can utilize to begin discovering your calling. These are strategies I addressed in my earlier book, but they're worth repeating here.

1. Ask yourself...

- What do you love to teach others?
- What do people compliment you on the most?
- What activity or topic of conversation energizes you?
- What activities do you do in your spare time or on a Saturday morning?
- If you won a billion dollars in the lottery, what would you choose to do with your life?

2. Ask family/friends...

You can also ask close friends and family about what you're good at. They can tell you quickly. You might even be surprised at what you hear. You could even ask your coworkers or boss.

Now, when you ask, make sure you give a reason, so they are truthful. What I mean by that is at times when asking close friends their opinion about you, the natural response is to be polite and tell you general things like, you're a nice person, you're friendly, courteous...blah, blah! These are very general things because they don't want to offend you. They are telling you what they think you want to hear. But what you want to know is more on your skills and talents.

That's why you'll want to give them a reason for why you're asking. Try something like, I'm working on a self-assessment project for work or a course. You could also say your boss or coach wants to know your strengths, gifts, etc. When people understand your intent or reason for your questions, they are more likely to give you honest feedback.

Some ideas for questions to ask:

- What would you say my strengths and gifts are?
- How would you describe me to someone else?
- Do you remember an incident where I did something that surprised and delighted you?
- How do I respond to challenges or conflicts?
- When have I been the happiest in my life?

3. Take an online personality test (optional)

There are plenty of free online resources to take advantage of. Below are the three most popular sites for the test that I have used personally

16personalities
Gallup strengths
Myers Briggs

If you work for a company, check with them, as they might offer free in-depth analysis for employees on some of these sites. Keep in mind that a personality test is taken just so you have a better understanding of how you like to work and the ways you work best. That includes your preferred communication style and even workplace environment.

Final thoughts...

So, can you become whatever you want to be (say, an engineer)? Yes. With enough study hours, practice, and application, you can do it.

But a better question to ask yourself is, is engineering is right for you? Is accounting right for you? Is a career in sales right for you?

Do you have any interest or curiosity in the field? But more importantly, does the job role enhance your gifted skill?

Also, just because you found your gift, doesn't mean that you're done! This doesn't factor in other important things like you getting fair pay, finding a good job environment, or being surrounded by people you enjoy working with.

These are all important and necessary to your success. However, you first need to know what you're good at before you can go for what you want. This is a starting point...remember, it's a journey.

I hope you find your gift, just as I did. Trust me, this won't be something you will find under the Christmas tree either.

"The two most important days of your life are the day you are born and the day you find out why." —Mark Twain

CHAPTER 8

Creating Vision

"Your vision will become clear only when you can consider your own heart. Who looks outside, dreams; who looks inside, awakes." —Carl Jung

AT THE BEGINNING OF this book, I mentioned that I won a prize for a free airline ticket to the USA, and later ended up moving there at age 21. Well, a lot of things happened in between winning the ticket and arriving in the USA. There was a gap of two to three years.

After winning the prize, I went to the US embassy in Harare to fill out my tourist visa application. This was around 2002. I remember my excitement and nervousness upon entering the building and approaching the visa interview. I couldn't believe it, I was one step closer to realizing my dream of visiting the USA. I already had the free airline ticket and accommodations.

As I proceeded to the waiting room inside the US embassy, I was a nervous wreck, my legs shook as I tried to swallow a big lump in my dry throat. I entered a small, cramped waiting area with around ten people all waiting their turn to be interviewed. As I sat there, I quickly realized the interview would be done at the window, out in the open in front of everyone.

This made me more nervous, not because I had something to hide, but because I'm a private person and not the type to share things out in the open. My heart was racing, and I felt the sweat in the palms of my hands as I tried to gather myself together. Then, suddenly, I hear my name called. Here it was—the moment of truth. One last hurdle between me and my life's dream.

We started the interview and I was immediately interrogated about why I wanted to go to the U.S., and so on. I felt it was more of an attack, as if I was wrong to visit the country.

At the time, it was assumed that people are applying as an illegal immigrant until they can prove to the embassy that they would be legal and come back to their country after visiting America. In other words, you're guilty until proven innocent. I did my interview a few months after the September 11, 2001, attacks, so the U.S. was much stricter on its immigration compared to previous years. To a degree, I sympathized and understood why they were tough, but at the same time, it still sucked for me. In the end, I was denied a visa on the spot due to not providing enough proof that I would come back home after visiting the U.S.

To say that I was devastated would be an understatement.

By the time I left the embassy, I was so down, depleted, and dejected. All the joy and excitement from earlier had disappeared.

I had told myself, "Just one more hurdle, you are so close." Only to have it snatched away in the blink of an eye.

Have you ever been so close to getting something you always wanted only to have it taken away from you at the last minute?

It's the hardest and worst feeling I had ever felt. It was an upsetting experience. It took a couple of weeks for me to recover. I kept asking how one person (the interviewer) could have the power to hold me back from what I wanted.

In the following months, I applied three more times for a visa and even a student visa upon receiving a scholarship to attend a U.S. college. All the requests were denied.

I gave it everything, and it was not good enough.

Do I give up or keep pushing? This couldn't be happening.

I reluctantly decided to go to South Africa for college at Rhodes University in Grahamstown. I was there for six months and failed my first semester miserably. It was my first time away from home without my family. I was not focused on my studies and was depressed a lot of the time from loneliness and disappointment. I remember watching mindless TV shows every day so that I could zone out and escape my reality.

During that period of my life, I thought nothing was going right for me.

After my first failed semester, I moved back home to Zimbabwe to rethink what I was going to do with my life. I still had the dream of going to the US, but I didn't know how to do it. I heard about the "Green Card Lottery" from family and friends in which the U.S. Immigration Department grants fifty thousand visas for people outside the USA to start a new life in America. I thought, what have I got to lose at this point if I enter.

Now, keep in mind that hundreds of millions of people apply for this visa lottery, so I knew I had a very small chance to win, but it was a chance nonetheless. I applied for it but went about my life planning for my next destination and didn't think about it again.

Two after my last rejection to go study in the USA, I decided to accept an offer to attend college at the University of Newcastle in Australia. Australia immigration was much more lenient than the USA immigration back then.

On the day I submitted my documents to the Australian embassy to begin processing my visa, I went home and found a large brown envelope sitting on my table that was mailed in.

I didn't recognize it, but it had my name on it. Part of me was excited to get a letter, but another part was curious about what this might be. Usually, the big envelopes I got were from US colleges with brochures and application forms for their universities. There would always be a university symbol or logo on the envelope. The envelope I was holding didn't have that.

Curious, I cut open the envelope. I pulled out a stack of papers that looked like application forms. As I began to read one of the letters, the first thing that caught my eye was, "Congratulations!" but I still didn't know what it was. As I read further, I found out I won the Green Card Lottery. In other words, I had been granted a permanent legal residence to start life in the USA.

What!?! That can't be right!

I thought it must be a scam or a joke.

I was always told that if it's too good to be true, then it's probably not true.

But as I looked through the paperwork, everything seemed legit. I even received the application forms for the local US embassy that I would have had to pay hundreds of dollars to obtain, but here I was holding them in my hands for free.

I asked myself, how could this be?

Then it hit me—I applied for the visa lottery a few years ago. I had completely forgotten that I had applied.

I was so excited and in complete shock. I stopped myself and thought, what about Australia? What do I do now? Do I stick to my plan to go there, or do I quit and take my chances on this US opportunity?

Have you ever been stuck between two equally good choices? Knowing that whatever decision you make will completely change your life's direction?

What are the odds that I would receive this letter on the same day I submitted the documents to leave for Australia?

Was this destiny or a sign?

I was at a crossroad. This was an important decision. I wanted to stick to my plan, but at the same time, my heart and gut were telling me to go to the USA. I still had the painful feeling of three US visa rejections in the back of my mind, so what if this would be the fourth rejection? I would be risking my opportunity in Australia that was already approved. I was 20 years old at the time, and I had already gone through so much rejection and disappointment chasing this dream. Could I do it one more time?

I decided to go for it.

The next day I went to the Australian embassy to ask for my documents back and cancel my visa application. The people at the embassy were shocked and puzzled by my request. I didn't tell them anything other than something came up, and I couldn't pursue that college anymore, but that I was grateful for receiving the opportunity.

A few weeks later, I went to do my interview at the US embassy. By then, I was confident and ready. I had already been rejected, so the fear of rejection no longer had a stranglehold on me.

It was my last chance, and I believed that it was my moment.

I hoped for the best but expected the worst. I went in for the fourth time to the US embassy and did my interview. I couldn't believe what happened next. I was approved right then and there! No rejection or denial—this time it was a complete turnaround.

I was over the moon. All the disappointment and pain I went through to finally realize this dream had paid off. I got the documents and left the embassy to tell my mum who was waiting for me in the car.

This whole experience taught me a big lesson and the value of perseverance.

You see, when you have a strong vision of what you want in your life and have the focus and determination to go after it, nothing can stop you. It's not easy, and I realized back then it was not supposed to be.

There were so many challenges and setbacks that came my way. Most of them came very close to the finish line. I wanted to give up, but something in me said, "Do it one more time." You will have fears and doubts, but your vision will give you the faith to proceed even when you're scared.

Creating your vision

What do you envision for your life?

What is your vision for your career, relationships, environment, etc.? What experiences are you looking for?

Do you take the time to sit and think about what your dream life would look like? Most people don't spend enough time in this area, and if you're not one of them, then consider yourself lucky. If you don't plan for your life, then somebody else will. There is always someone who will tell you to "do this career" or "start that business" or "live in this country."

But nobody can tell you what your vision can look like because it's a personal and a unique journey designed for you, by you. Therefore, it is so critical you begin today to create your vision.

There are a thousand directions that you can go in your life. So many careers, environments, people, or life paths to take. I could've gone to Australia and not the USA. Then again, I could've gone anywhere in the world to start a new life.

Why couldn't I just go to England or Asia for college? It would have been easier. Why go through all the pain and suffering to go to the USA? Because it was my dream. It was my vision. That's the difference. I tried South Africa, and it didn't work out because that was not my path. When you create a vision and pursue it, that is what will give your life fulfillment.

What path are you taking right now?

Is it one that was given to you or one that was chosen by you?

The cost of not dreaming

The most significant challenge most people have is creating goals before they begin to develop a vision. I know this was my biggest weakness after arriving in the USA. You see, I had fulfilled my vision coming to the USA and graduating college. Then I made a big mistake. I stopped dreaming. I failed to create my next vision. I followed everyone's advice about my life path to start a career and start making lots of money.

I began to lead a comfortable life. I was going after finance jobs because I graduated in the subject and knew a little bit about it. In fact,

I went into finance because others suggested it. Since I had nothing planned for myself, I just followed what others expected of me.

I started my career, moved up the corporate ladder, and worked for some of the largest companies in the US. I was getting paid well, but I wasn't happy or fulfilled in my roles. Every time I had a new job position, I was bored after a few months and wanted to make a change.

I changed jobs many times, hoping to find that right one that would give me the long-lasting challenge and fulfillment I needed.

I didn't have a vision for my career.

I defined success by how much money I made. I would chase the next opportunity, and if the pay was higher, then that's what I was going to do.

Not once did I stop to ask myself if I even liked finance. The honest answer was no. Not once did I wake up and say, "I can't wait to do financial analytics and work on spreadsheets all day."

I began to redefine success in my life.

I started to define it not by how much money I made, but rather by how happy I was. This shifted my whole view on my career and life decisions.

I began to ask different questions:

- What do I want for my career? What would be my dream job?
- What skills am I looking to improve upon?
- How will this job add to my success in the long run?

I stopped dreaming after I arrived to the USA and graduated college and so I got comfortable with life and didn't set a higher vision for myself.

As a result, the last few years led me to a career and life where I was unfulfilled in what I was doing. I followed a path that was designed by others, pursuing it despite the disappointments I felt.

Therefore, I do urge you to create a vision for yourself that's aligned to you. There are thousands of directions that you can go forward in your life, but there's only one that will give you that fulfillment. That one direction is the one you choose on your own. No one can give you advice or direct you because the vision comes from your inner being. It's unique to you.

To help you with your vision, you'll find a few questions below so you can begin to create the masterpiece of your life.

Questions:

1. Write a one-page description of where you would like to be in your career and life in the next six months or year.
2. Look forward three to five years and have a vision of your ideal future.
3. List the steps can you take immediately to begin turning your future vision into your current reality.

Please spend however long you need to complete the questions. It might take you an hour, a few hours, or a few days. There's no rush, as these are not easy questions to answer. They require you to go within yourself to understand what you truly want.

Alternative method:

If you're struggling with the above exercise, here is another way to begin creating the vision you want in your life. Ask yourself:

Why do I want to pursue the goals that I have?

Are you pursuing your current goals because society (family, friends, mentor) told you to do so? Getting that comfortable, respectable job to make everyone happy?

Remember, you can only be who you are, and who you are right now may not be who you're intended to be.

I made the mistake of listening to others instead of my gut.

The people who advised me meant well, but unfortunately, that advice was based on their beliefs on what I was capable of and not mine. Don't let this be you. Again, I ask:

- Why do you want the goals you set?
- What do you hope to accomplish with your goal? In other words, what experiences are you hoping to get out of it?
- If you had all the money and time in the world (no constraints), what would you be doing?

These are questions to think about as you begin to create your vision and will get you straight to the source of what you want—if you are honest with yourself.

Quick, Five-Minute Exercise:

Below is another way to approach creating your vision. Please spend only five minutes answering the questions below. The time constraint will force you to write as quickly as you can, without thinking too much. Usually the first thought (or instinct) that comes to mind will tell you your real desires.

So, as you answer these questions, just write down whatever pops into your head without judging or overthinking.

Are you ready? Let's go. Timer on.

- Where do you see yourself living in the next few years? What environment are you surrounded by?
- Who are you with? Family, friends, work colleagues?
- Where are you traveling around the world?
- What type of work are you doing?
- What type of health do you have? How does your body look, and what foods are you eating?
- What car are you driving?
- How do you want to contribute to the world? Is it through writing, volunteering, monetary donation?
- What type of person do you want to be? What values or character do you want to embody?

I hope you gained some valuable insight from these vision exercises. This might be the most important chapter in the book as you create your dream life. I can't begin to tell you how answering these simple, yet powerful questions changed my life's direction and how I prioritize my hours, days, weeks, months, and years.

CHAPTER 9

The Immense Power of Intention

"C'MON, WHAT'S ONE MORE going to hurt?"

Has that statement ever been said to you by any of your friends or family members?

You start a new diet, and the next day you are out with a few friends at a café, and you hear "C'mon, one slice of chocolate of cake is not going to hurt. You live only once, right? Don't be a party pooper."

Well, this happened to me recently.

I was at a restaurant with a few friends. I happened to be on a weight loss program and had lost about ten pounds in three months, so I was cautious about what I ate, especially when going out and socializing with a group.

We all had a good time and ate a great meal. I was full after eating my favorite Irish dish, Shepherd's pie. I was so proud I had not indulged in the warm, steamy baked bread that accompanied our dishes.

The server came to check on us at the end and asked, "Would you all like dessert?" Everyone said yes, except me. I used to feel awkward or uncomfortable being the odd one out, but I worked too hard to mess up what I had accomplished with my weight loss.

Suddenly everyone at the table was pressuring me to eat dessert. I resisted at first, but slowly I started to talk myself into eating cake.

I was justifying it to myself. "Yeah, why not have one? Plus, in the grand scheme of things, it won't hurt my progress."

I saw myself moving slowly toward the dark side and just saying yes to cheesecake. But I held my ground, until the menu came across my face and I saw the list of cheesecakes with all different flavors from blueberries to red velvet. Suddenly, I no longer felt full and had room for dessert. I was practically salivating over the thought of a slice of cheesecake.

Then my friend turned to me and said something that stopped me in my tracks.

"C'mon, what's one piece of cake going to do?"

I paused at that moment and realized something. Those are the same words I'd been telling myself for a long time.

What's one more going to hurt?

One more donut, one more pizza, one more burger. I mean, when you think about it, "one more" seems harmless, right?

How can this one bite hurt? The truth is not much will happen in the moment. But at the same time, it only takes one bite to start a habit. Regardless if it's a good or bad habit. You might never have drunk coffee, but it just takes one cup of coffee to start you on your way. Then another cup, then a third and fourth cup, and next thing you know you have a coffee addiction.

By the way, not every addiction is inherently bad. I drink coffee occasionally, and coffee is a significant part of my Ethiopian culture. The point is that it takes one to get to two or more cups.

I now understand how addicts become addicts. Nobody just wakes up and becomes one. It takes time to build a constant habit of an unhealthy behavior. Sometimes you don't realize it until someone says "just one more."

On the other hand, one more could be a good thing. You can build good habits. If you're starting to write a book, you can say, "What's writing one more page going to hurt?" Just one. Not two, three, five, or ten pages, but just one. Guess what. That one page will multiply to two, then three, then the next thing you know you have twenty pages, and you now have a good habit and you're on your way to becoming an author.

It takes one step to begin a journey of one thousand miles. It takes one person to inspire a movement of thousands.

It takes losing one pound before you can lose twenty pounds. Just one...

Building good habits can lead to your future success and help maintain your high-level confidence and self-esteem.

Confidence doesn't just appear; you must build it up.

You can create rituals or habits that set you up for success. As I built up more confidence in myself every day, my self-esteem and how I viewed myself improved. I started getting bolder and getting out of my comfort zone more. I stopped self-sabotaging and made more progress toward my goals.

Before I knew it, I made more progress in one year than I had over the last six years. I learned that life transformation doesn't happen in a single moment or show up because of one event; Instead, it's a series of small events before the change. Life transformation is a series of excellent habits that once you incorporate into your daily routine, turn into significant transformation over time.

It's like the snowball effect. When the small snowball starts rolling down the mountain, you won't see it because it's small, but as it continues down the hill, it begins to grow and build momentum. As it approaches the base of the mountain, you now notice the change and how that small snowball transformed into a giant ball. The same idea applies to transformation in any area of your life.

If you want to change careers, you need to start putting good habits into learning a new skill. If you're going to improve your relationships, you need to develop better habits in communicating with others. Over time, you will develop new skills and change careers. You will have better, deeper, more fulfilled relationships and be more appreciative of others.

Goals without plans are just dreams

Hopefully you have your vision/goals already written down from the previous chapter. If not, please consider going back to review and write them down. It is essential to understand that your goals should align with your vision. It's like driving on a long journey from the east coast to west coast. You see yourself arriving in California (your vision), and your goals are like the mile-marker signs along the way telling you how far you have left to your destination. It is a signal of whether you're moving toward or away from your vision. It is the validation that you're getting closer to realizing your dreams

Create a clear Goal Statement

Begin by writing down a goal that's tied to your vision. To create your vision statement just follow the below steps in creating an effective goal affirmation. Let's use weight loss as an example.

A. Realistic

Make sure your goals are realistic and specific. Don't jump ahead of your current abilities and say you will work out every day for one hour when you have never worked out for longer than twenty or thirty minutes a few times a week.

Not realistic: *"To work out every day for one hour."*

Realistic: *"To do regular exercise for thirty minutes a day, at least four times a week."*

B. Measurable

Make your goals measurable. How else will you know if you're making progress toward your goals if you don't measure or track them? If you're losing weight, you can weigh yourself on the scale or use a tape measure to check for progress. Check in with yourself regularly and make sure that you are moving forward.

Not measurable: *"I want to lose a few pounds."*

Measurable: *"I want to lose twenty pounds."*

We can break this one down a bit further. So, let's say I want to lose twenty pounds in four months. That means I will need to lose five pounds a month. Five pounds is the milestone for the first month and losing ten pounds is the milestone for the second month and so on. This is helpful because if I don't lose five pounds in the first month, then next month I need to make up for it and work extra hard. Not meeting realistic goals can mean that it is time to try a different approach in reaching them.

C. Set a deadline

Setting a deadline adds a sense of urgency that will help pull you toward the finish line. Time is limited, and the most successful among us set deadlines so that they will not waste either their time or energy.

Now it might be easy to be flexible and call your progress "good enough" when you get close to the end of a deadline, but I urge you to hold off and keep pushing. You never know what you're capable of completing. You might just make it.

No set deadline: *"I want to lose twenty pounds by next year."*

Set deadline: *"I want to lose twenty pounds by June 6th."*

Let's put it all together with the A+B+C goal structure. Also, make sure the statement is in present tense (as if it's a current fact).

Goal Statement:

I am twenty pounds smaller in body weight by June 6, 2019.

There it is.

You just created a powerful yet straightforward goal statement or affirmation. It's not wishy-washy. You're clear on exactly what you want, and you have a framework for getting there.

The "I am" statement at the beginning is powerful because it communicates to your brain that it is a fact. Once you begin to believe it, you will slowly start to see it.

Hint: Write down your goals on paper. Writing them down leaves a powerful impression on your mind. The act of physically writing them on paper (not typing them into an app) employs multiple senses. It allows you to see them on paper with your eyes. You feel the paper in your hand. They become tangible and no longer just an idea in your head. All this makes a powerful impression in your mind to record and keep it in your subconscious mind.

Using focus to help you achieve your dreams

"You can focus on things that are barriers, or you can focus on scaling the wall or redefining the problem." —Tim Cook

Nothing of substance has been accomplished without a deliberate focus on the desired outcome. When you focus on what you hope for, you will begin to attract the people, opportunities, and scenarios that lead you toward success.

Your brain is wired for goal-seeking, and it needs a target to aim for. To help understand the importance of focusing on what's important to you, I want to talk quickly about a concept called "RAS."

RAS (Reticular Activating System)

Most people in the personal development world know of this term. It is basically how our minds focus on things that are important in our lives as we go about on our day-to-day view of our environment. Our brain processes lots of information (millions of data) at any given moment—from what we see to what we hear all around us. Now, it is impossible for us to focus on every little detail in our environment. We would go crazy! The RAS allows you to focus on a few things in your surroundings that match your interests and priorities.

A common example is when you buy a new car, e.g. a Ford Focus. You would have never noticed the car on the road before, but since you bought the car you notice it everywhere.

Why is that?

Is it because the car dealership coincidentally had a huge sale and everyone in your city is now driving a similar car? Most likely not. The reason you suddenly notice it everywhere is that you have placed that particular car as an important part of your life (subconsciously, at least), so when you look to the world, your brain scans and brings to your attention Ford cars on the streets. There may be a hundred cars (different brands/models) that you're looking at in any given moment, but you will detect the Ford very quickly. If you had another person next to you who owned a Toyota, you might be surprised that he/she would not detect the Ford but would quickly point out the nearest Toyota.

So why is this important?

If you want to go for your goals in life and you want to attract the right people, situations, and even luck, you want your mind to focus and help you detect anything that is aligned with your vision or goals.

Your mind is like a heat-seeking missile system. It goes and seeks a target to which it wants to place its focus on. For example, if your goal is to write a book, then you will quickly notice anything in the world that mentions a book in the headline and pay attention to it.

FOCUS in the moment

By that, I mean to be in the moment.

In the past, I never quite understood what that meant. If I'm living and standing here, am I not present with you?

But I learned the difference between being here and being present. It all comes down to focus. Focus on where you are right now, giving your full attention to the present. Your mind is clear, not thinking about the future or past but just the here and now.

Just because your body is here and you're looking at someone doesn't mean you're present. Sometimes you just zone out. Or maybe you're like I was—while someone else was talking, I was already preparing a response in the back of my mind when I should have been listening to the other person.

Get out of your head and become aware of what's happening around you. I remember I was such a worried person before participating in a conversation with someone or a group or just going out in public. I over-analyzed everything. How someone looked, spoke, or reacted to something. I was overly critical of how I spoke and looked. Is my posture correct? Do I need to raise my voice? Am I too loud? What do I say next? Is he or she judging me?

It was paralyzing, and by the time I was done with social events, I was completely exhausted. My brain fried from all the analyzing. Going to job interviews were the worst for me because when I went in, I had already prepared my answers to possible questions. I memorized the answers word-for-word because I was afraid I would freeze up. If the interviewer asked anything that was out of the ordinary, I would be clueless and just freeze. As you can imagine, it would quickly become an awkward moment.

I always needed a plan before I did anything. I never allowed spontaneity to enter my decisions or life. That's because I was never truly in the moment. I did not pick up on social cues or nonverbal clues that people were communicating because I was stuck inside my head, overthinking my next move. I avoided making eye contact with anyone because I was just that uncomfortable.

It was once I began to embrace imperfection that I slowly let go of trying to please everyone. When I no longer planned everything and could go into a situation confident, I got my desired result and could respond to whatever came my way. There are many times that I will be asked a unique question on the spot, and I now respond with whatever comes to me intuitively. Of course, I make mistakes, but it's never the end of the world.

What's important is that I live in the moment and focus on that, not what might happen or not.

So, do you live in the moment?

Being present is important because that's where the beauty of life is—not your past or future, just here and now. You'll notice small details in your day, like the birds singing in a nearby tree. You may have walked that path to work many times and not noticed that funny billboard next to your office building, even though it has been there for months.

You can get so caught up with things that you never stop just to breathe and be present. Clear your head. Maybe you're still angry at a driver that cut you off in traffic or worried about a work project you need to present next week. Stop allowing those thoughts to steal your focus from the present.

Being present is not about forgetting your past or ignoring your future or even ignoring how you feel, it's embracing the joy of just being there. To be observant of life and everything around you. To love yourself as human and embrace how you feel without letting it overwhelm you.

I know what you're thinking, that it is easier said than done, right? Well, I never said it would be easy.

FOCUS on gratitude

Being grateful is one of the most powerful keys to living a happy and fulfilled life. Gratitude allows you to be present. You can't be grateful and angry at the same time. At times, I would have a "scarcity" mindset where I would worry that I didn't have enough money to pay this bill or worry about a project, telling myself I was not doing enough when I was already giving 100%. You can change the thought of "not enough" to I'm "full." You can begin to have an abundance mindset vs. a scarcity mindset.

Every morning I write down five things I'm grateful for in my life. I started this a year ago, and it has made me more balanced and appreciative of the little things in my life. If a large bill came to me, I would stress out and blame everyone for my stress. I had the mindset of, I don't have enough money, even though that is not the case. Now when I get a bill, I'm grateful that I have the money to pay it. If the internet bill comes, I'm grateful that I pay the company to provide internet so I can communicate with friends and family.

I even practice gratitude before any social gathering so my mind is in the right place. It's funny because I might go to an event with a few friends and we each will have different experiences from it.

For example, the other day I was in a restaurant with two friends. We arrived at 8 PM at a Chinese restaurant to get a table and ended up waiting thirty minutes before being seated. When we were seated, the waiter came and took our order. It was only forty-five minutes before they closed, and it was apparent he was in a rush to take our orders and get the food out quickly.

One of my friends didn't like the waiter and felt he was rude, annoying, and disrespectful. I didn't think anything of it and was just grateful to go out with my friends. I was thankful to find a beautiful place to eat that was still open. I was grateful I had money to pay the check and have a nice meal with friends.

Now, this is not to say that the waiter was not rude and pushy. He probably was, and my friends were probably right. But I didn't notice it. I was grateful for everything around me and the details that mattered to me. What you focus on, is what you manifest (the RAS effect).

Try noticing the power of your focus and how it can impact your experience at any given moment. Before you go into a situation, phone call, environment, what is your intention? Whatever intention you set before a meeting or conversation will help to manifest the outcome you want.

FOCUS on small wins

You need to practice small, daily courage-builders, so you can be prepared for when you really need it for the big challenges. Courage doesn't have to be reserved only for the big decisions in your life.

It could be as simple as:

- saying 'no' to a work colleague or boss who's asking you to take on an additional workload that you can't manage right now.
- Saying 'no' to a friend who invited you to a party because you just finished a 12-hour shift at work and you're exhausted.
- telling your spouse or boyfriend/girlfriend that you don't like the way they treat you at certain times.

It takes courage to speak up. Most of us have a fear of rejection from someone you care about deeply. Maybe at work you have a fear that if you don't do this or that you will get fired or won't be up for that promotion or the boss won't favor you for great opportunities.

Not only is this not true, but you're hurting yourself in the long run by not using the opportunity to grow your strength.

It takes courage to express how you honestly feel and be vulnerable.

I remember when I started a new job for a large company, I had a lot of deadlines that I needed to meet for projects. It was very stressful and high-pressure. I was the new guy, and I felt I had to show my worth. So, any work assignments that my manager threw at me, I made sure to take it, even though I was already working on multiple projects. I didn't want him to think I was lazy or incompetent. At the same time, I was stressed, overworked, and exhausted every day.

One day he was about to give me additional work but this time he told me, "Don't say yes because I'm asking you to do this. Only agree if you can make room for this additional work in your already full to-do list." I was surprised and relieved he said that. I told him I had a lot on my plate and didn't think I could handle another project at that time. He was okay with it and assigned the work to someone else. That was an enlightenment for me, to say 'no' without feeling guilty about it. As a people-pleaser, I always felt the pressure to say 'yes,' even to things I couldn't or didn't want to do at the moment. People might get upset with you for saying 'no,' but what I've learned is they will respect you more for standing up and being honest.

FOCUS on building your self-confidence

Self-confidence is not something we catch or are born with, but instead, it's something we build up. Whenever you try to do something new, your confidence will be low at first. However, over time as you practice and get familiar with the activity, you will start to build up confidence. You begin to see and predict patterns and know how to react accordingly.

When I started interviewing for jobs in America, I was terrible (and I knew it too). I didn't know how to communicate with managers or recruiters. But after practicing and lots of interviews, I slowly began to relax and learn from my mistakes. I built up my confidence, and now, years later, I can do interviews more easily because I know how to prepare and what to say.

If this once-timid kid from Africa who struggled to communicate to American employers can now confidently master interviews and so many other scenarios that I feared, you can too. So again, build your confidence through practice in whatever area you want to head toward.

A trick I learned is to keep a small note card of some (or all) of your accomplishments in your life. This is so helpful because you want to have reminders of your past successes to keep you pushing forward. You might be scared in the moment, but you have overcome challenges far more significant than what you're currently facing.

Some things to consider writing down:

What have you accomplished in the last three years? It can be anything and doesn't have to have a monetary value.

A time when you felt lucky or special. (I'm not referring to when your mum tells you you're a special child, not the same thing here.)

What has been your happiest moment in life? What struggle did you overcome?

My happiest moments are when I:

- *Received the US immigration letter that I would have the opportunity to start life in the USA.*
- *Graduated from a US college, and my mum and sister traveled halfway around the world to attend the ceremony.*

- *Got my first job offer at my ideal company to start a finance career, after being rejected from them ten times.*
- *Published my first book after spending months writing it and years procrastinating.*

Now, your list doesn't have to look like mine. It could be as simple as being told by someone that you have an eye for fashion or you are an amazing artist. Maybe an accomplishment is finding the love of your life and marrying him or her. It could be overcoming a lousy situation (family member's death, sickness, etc.) or quitting a job you hated.

"I don't focus on what I'm up against. I focus on my goals and I try to ignore the rest." —Venus Williams

Conclusion

THE HARDEST PART OF my transformation was not when I quit a job where I was miserable, or cut off from bad relationships, or even publishing my first book. The hardest part was believing that I could do those things. Knowing that I could take a risk and have faith that there was something better for me on the other side, even though I didn't know what it was. The believing that everything would work out all right by having faith in myself.

Don't be held hostage to the belief that you can't do better than you are now.

Before this transformative process, I had always followed the saying that "seeing is believing." I learned that's not true. BELIEVING IS SEEING.

If you believe in the possibilities and work towards them, you will see them come true eventually. You must visualize it in your mind first before you can see it in the real world.

When I was younger, I always imagined coming to the USA to start life and go to school. I accomplished it, and I will never take that for granted. It began with me seeing myself living that life. I faced a lot of challenges, rejections, and heartbreaks, but it was all well worth it.

Have the dream of what you want first—then move toward it. If you fail along the way, that's okay. Adjust your path but don't give up on the dream.

Everything you see in front of you, whether it's a cell phone, computer, car, plane, etc., all started in someone's mind. Someone had a thought that led to an idea and the imagination of possibilities. For example, innovators like Steve Jobs helped create a whole new way of listening to music and communicating with each other. It all starts with a thought before it's an idea, which later becomes reality as you pursue your idea.

Humans are emotional creatures and every action we take in life is based on our interpretation of an event that in turn affects how we feel. The secret to transformation is embracing your emotions. The good, the bad and the ugly emotions. That's it!

One of the biggest mistakes I made was not being aware of or acknowledging how I felt. When I would feel any negativity in my body, I would numb it or just ignore it. Then I learned that numbing a feeling does not last. It will come up again waiting for your strength to meet it head-on. It's like a small virus in the body that slowly kills your inner self unless you let it go.

I am an introvert, or maybe I should say I have been an introvert. My transformation is continually taking me outside of that self-limiting box as well. There is a part of me that is outgoing and wants to express myself boldly, while the other part also loves the strong introverted side of myself. Maybe I am a social introvert. Can we only be one thing? Should we limit ourselves by labeling ourselves?

There is a favorite phrase of that says, "To be someone that you have never been before, you will have to do things that you've never done before." It is all part of the transformation process, and you need to be able to manage these feelings when they pop up in order to move forward even when you're scared or fearful.

The human mind is powerful, and it's designed to make all of us successful. There is no need to move states or countries, change jobs or relationships to transform your life. All that's needed is to first change your perspective.

Remember, when you change your beliefs, you change your reality.

Take full responsibility for your life and all your decisions. No more blaming others or making excuses for why you're not succeeding.

Find your clique

Don't go it alone; have a community around you for accountability as you go ahead to accomplish your goals. Better yet, hire a coach or get a mentor to guide you on your journey. It changed my life. Do you have to pay a price? Yes, but it's worth the investment. It's an investment in yourself. Having someone beside you who has been where you want to go will help you get there faster.

There will be voices outside of you, whether family or friends, telling you that you can't do it. That you can't go for that crazy dream of yours.

Who do you think you are? Why don't you be realistic?

Are you sure you want to risk it?

One of these comments coming from someone you trust or admire can set you back days, weeks, months, or even years from moving toward your goals. That's why it's so important to be surrounded by a community of empowering voices that keep inspiring you to move forward. To lift you up when you fall. To help you drown your negative thoughts, doubts, and fears. To hold you accountable.

*"If you want to go fast, go alone.
If you want to run farther, do it together."
—African Proverb*

Harvest your rewards

CONGRATULATIONS on reaching this far in the book!

You have the seeds for success to go after your dreams. Now you need to create the foundation in which to add the seeds so that you can grow and harvest your rewards.

Focus on exactly what you want in your life.

Any daily tasks that are not moving you closer to your goals need to be put aside. Simple!

Whenever you're doing a job or task, ask yourself, will this activity bring me closer to my vision?

I would like to leave you with my favorite quote:

"Rather be prepared and not get an opportunity, than to get an opportunity and not be prepared." —Les Brown

About the Author

PETROS ESHETU IS AN Ethiopian author (INTJ specifically). He was born in Italy, but spent most of his life in Harare, Zimbabwe, living there through high school before fulfilling his dream at age 21 of starting his life in America.

Upon graduating college and working in corporate America for a few years, Petros became disillusioned with some aspects of his life.

He decided to answer a question that had been at the center of his thoughts for many years. What is my passion and purpose? Who am I? He was tired of being someone he was not. Tired of seeking approval from others.

Having spent many months researching, studying, and learning from mentors, he transformed his life and became an author and a book writing coach.

In his spare time, Petros enjoys an obsession with reading and visiting bookstores. He also loves to indulge himself by trying out new cafés and restaurants and traveling the world to visit his far-flung family and friends while exploring new places.

You can contact Petros at petros@petroseshetu.com or you can find him at www.petroseshetu.com.

REVIEW REQUEST

It will mean the world to me if you could leave a review on Amazon so other people can also discover this book. Even if it's just writing 1 or 2 sentences.

Thank you so much!

www.ingramcontent.com/pod-product-compliance
Lightning Source LLC
Chambersburg PA
CBHW070521100426
42743CB00010B/1900